How to Get Over Anyone in A Few Days

Breakups Will Never Hurt Like Before

Contents

About the Author

M. Farouk Radwan is the founder of one of the most popular self-help websites on the internet in terms of traffic. www.2knowmyself.com, the site Farouk founded, was getting more than one million visits a month at the time this book was published.

Farouk has been studying psychology since he was 17 years old. He has completed several psychology-related degrees, written thousands of articles and authored 10 books.

In 2012, Farouk announced becoming a 'dot com millionaire' after he had sold more than 1,000,000 dollars of his psychology books and products online.

Farouk doesn't believe in intuitive tricks or perceptive advice, but he rather focuses on methods that have been proven to be 100% practical through scientific research, and that are backed up by scientific fact.

About the Co-Author

Reem Ismail is a passionate and dynamic self-development coach. She trains people all around the world to enhance their skills of using their subconscious mind to achieve their goals. She has stated her mission-statement to be, "Using my energetic and motivational spirit – in addition to ample information and experience in human development and psychology – to help others face their challenges, feel happy, and realize their dreams in all areas of their personal and professional life."

Coaching people from many different cultures and countries around the world such as the US, Canada, the UK, Australia, Russia, South Africa, Morocco, Egypt, China, and India, Ismail has gained extensive experience in how to deal with different people and train them, regardless of their different mindsets.

She is a regular guest on TV shows, sharing information on various human development topics.

Testimonials

"Less than twelve hours have passed since my breakup and I am recovering already!"
-- **Fahmy Mo.**

"I have purchased your first 2 books, 'How to Make Someone Fall in Love With You' and 'How to Get Over Anyone in a Few Days.' I have found them to be the most powerful books that I have ever come across."
-- **Vickie**

"Of all the books I've read about this issue, I've never seen anything so powerful."
-- **Mira Essam**

"Your book helped me find answers to endless questions. It could have saved me years of anguish, had I read it sooner. Your book gave me scientific insight into breakups, while other books provided me with nothing but untested suggestions. I actually felt physically better as well as being mentally and emotionally cured of depression. Your book explained things so simply and honestly. I now view all the processes of love such as finding love, being loved, and recovering from losing love through a new, healthy spectrum. I am so much happier after reading your book."
-- **R.S**

"I want to thank you because your book was really helpful; it helped me do what I had been unable to do for a month in just 2 days."
-- **Riham Nour**

"I've been enduring emotional pain because of a break up for almost a year now and I thought I was the only one, but when I read this book, I found an answer to every 'Why' that had been occupying my mind.. It was my lucky day when I found your website after lots of research. I sincerely thank you!"
-- **Anonymous**

Warning

If you believe that falling in love is a process that inevitably involves emotional pain, suffering or heartache, you should be beware of the fact that if you decide to read this book, your response to breakups will be dramatically altered.

Those breakups that used to cause you to be depressed for months in the past will only upset you for a few days before you completely forget about them. Your attitude in your coming relationships won't be negatively affected; you will still experience loving emotions towards your next partners, but you will be able to prevent a breakup from ruining your life.

When you are done reading this book, you will be able to enjoy your love-life, but if one of your relationships comes to an end, you will be able to survive the breakup. My book will help you get rid of all of the false beliefs about relationships which the media has instilled in your mind; you will know the truth instead of being misled by the widespread myths about love.

Sharing your happiness or sadness with someone will make you happier or sadder, respectively. This is exactly what happens in a healthy relationship. However, when the relationship becomes a source of pain and suffering, you should know how to transform it into a healthy one.

There Are Rules

I claim that this is the best book there is tackling the topic of breakup recovery. If you happen to find a better reference anywhere else on the entire planet, please feel free to contact me and I will make sure that this introduction is modified.

Years ago, before I had good knowledge about the psychology of falling in love, I used to believe that for every person on this planet there is only one other person whom he/she could call "the one." I used to think that finding "Mr. /Ms. Right" would magically solve all your problems and make your life beautiful.

Like billions of other people, I thought that once you fall in love with someone, it would be impossible to leave that person and fall in love with someone else. However, gaining more knowledge about this topic was an eye-opener for me.

Now, breakups still hurt me, but only for a week, and sometimes for less than that. My expectations of love and relationships are realistic, which is fundamentally why I can have long-lasting relationships.

I am no exception to the rule, but I just happened to know the rules for having a thriving love-life. You will have exactly the same eye-opening experience right after you finish reading this book. It is intricately structured, so make sure you read it well and give proper thought to each of the concepts mentioned.

About the Book

You have made a great choice deciding to read this book. It is by far the most powerful guide in the world to getting over someone. This book is not simply different from other books that tackle the same subject, but is rather incomparable to them.

This book will make the worst breakup become a shock that you can recover from in a few weeks, if not days. Personally, I can get over the worst breakup in three days, but this is not how I used to be; breakups had the power to devastate me and keep me depressed for months until I gained knowledge about the psychology of love. This book intends to transfer to you this knowledge that can make you forget about anyone in a few days.

The information provided in my book is backed up by science, not personal opinion. It is very well-phrased and presented to help you understand how you can overcome traumatic breakups. While reading it, you will find practical information rather than pieces of wise-sounding pieces of advice that are hard to apply. After reading it, breakups will never cause you as much distress as they used to do in the past.

A few days after applying the tips I offer you, you will start to feel better. By the second week, you will have recovered by up to 50%, your mood will have started to improve, and you will feel particularly lighthearted. The only thing you have to do is to stick to what the book tells you.

While reading, you will not only gain information on how to get over someone, but you will also gain insights into how to live a healthy and prosperous life. Once you finish reading my book, you will have gained valuable knowledge about psychology and the workings of your mind that will have a great impact on your life.

What Is Love?

Let's start off by trying to understand what love is and how it happens. Defining the most important aspect of any situation usually gives us a clearer understanding and better insight into the situation, and hence allows us to act wisely on it.

Try to picture the following scenario. Sam was feeling happy on his way to school when he suddenly met John who bullied him, took his wallet and made fun of him in front of everyone. Sam, however, wasn't bothered and went on with his day normally.

The next day, John met Sam and bullied him again. Sam nevertheless ignored this episode of humiliation and forgave John. But on the third day, Sam was bullied by John again.

Sam went home that day feeling humiliated and went straight to sleep. While Sam was asleep, his subconscious mind was awake, thinking about what had happened to him over the past three days. The following was the sequence of thoughts that passed through Sam's subconscious mind:

- Why is John doing this? I feel really humiliated.
- I need to find a solution to stop this from happening again.
- Tomorrow, I will beat John up in front of everyone so that he'll stop bullying me. But mind you, John is triple my size and does boxing, so how can I do that?
- It looks like there is no other option but to avoid him.

At this point, Sam's mind concludes that since John can't be beaten, it's better to find a way to avoid him. So how can Sam's mind guarantee that he won't have to deal with John again? A feeling of intense dislike is aroused in Sam whenever he sees John, which makes him refrain from dealing with him. In other words, Sam's subconscious mind has made him hate John so that he will avoid him in the future.

Therefore, hatred is nothing more than a mechanism used by your subconscious mind to make sure that you will stay away from those who harm you or pose a threat to your well-being.

Now, suppose that every time John bullied Sam, Sarah told Sam that she thought John was a rude person, while Sam is kind. Over the course of a few days, Sam's subconscious mind will start realizing that Sarah makes him feel happy, and thus it will think of a way of bringing him closer to her. As you may already have guessed, the method that Sam's subconscious mind will use to stay close to Sarah is nothing other than the emotion of love.

Thus, love can be defined as a method used by your subconscious mind to bring you closer to the people who boost your self-love or those who can enhance your emotional well-being.

The question you might be asking yourself is, "If this story is true, I can make anyone fall in love with me simply by being nice to him/her, can't I? But the answer to that is, "No, you can't." This is a common misconception. You can make someone fall in love with you only if you both treat that person well and meet his/her "subconscious criteria," which is a check-list of the qualities we desire in our dream partners embedded in our minds. Just treating a person nicely would make that person see you as a good friend, but not necessarily a good romantic partner.

The "unconscious criteria" is the topic that will be tackled in the following chapter, but let's first uncover more truths about love. Given the story above, it can be deduced that the emotions we experience are messages from our subconscious mind telling us to do something.

Seen in that light, depression would be a signal encouraging you to try to solve your problems. If you ignore it, you would enter into worse stages of depression, which are the brain's way of sending you more urgent signals.

If you meet someone who your brain believes to be a good match for you, it will send you love emotions to make you become attached to that person.

Many people like to give love in order to get love. The reason behind this human tendency is that when their brains perceive the love you give people as something desirable, they receive signals of love emotion because they consider your presence in their lives as being favorable.

In the field of body language, it is commonly known that one of the best ways to create a rapport with people is to smile. When you smile at people, you exude positive feelings which make them feel elated and comfortable. If your smile is not interpreted in any way other than kindness, they will smile back at you or feel happy to be around you.

Further on, you will learn more about the two main kinds of love and why they happen. Identifying them and learning more about them will help you see the concept of love in a better light, and thus deal with it wisely. It will also help you identify your fallback positions when it comes to your attitude towards love.

The Unconscious Criteria

Your past experiences, backgrounds, values and beliefs are the four constitutions that are brought together by your subconscious mind in order to make up the criteria that anyone must meet before you fall in love with him/her.

Imagine this scenario: A five-year-old girl notices that most of her friends at school have a nice toy that lights up and makes different shapes as it spins round.

Being amused by the toy, the little girl excitedly tells her parents how fantastic it is and asks them to buy her one. Sadly, however, her parents tell her that they don't have enough money to buy her the toy.

As the girl was growing up many of her wishes were denied in the same way because her parents' financial status was deteriorating. Her desire to be on the same social level as her school friends was continually frustrated.

Later on, her parents fell into debt and could barely provide her with her basic material needs. That is when they asked her to learn to become financially independent.

To a fifteen-year-old girl, this seemed a great burden. In addition, she had to go through great emotional turmoil, watching her parents struggling with financial insecurity and living from hand to mouth.

Although she learned how to provide for herself, she had developed fears of being penniless which would haunt her for the rest of her life. Now if this girl met an affluent man, she would most probably feel attracted to him. Being well to do and willing to provide for her has become one of the criteria according to which she will choose her partner.

Our beliefs, fears, values and criteria are a product of the circumstances in which we grew up, whether easy or difficult, whether created by our parents, or by other influences.

In other words, one of the factors determining the people we might fall in love with is our past experiences. If you take that into consideration, you may not feel as distressed when someone rejects you; your rejecter may want someone else other than you because of a childhood experience which has made their criteria demand something you do not have.

Unless you meet a person's subconscious criteria, or at least part of them, he/she will never fall in love you, and unless someone meets your subconscious criteria you can never fall in love with him/her.

Only in special cases discussed in my book "How to Make Someone Fall in Love with you," can someone compromise some of their subconscious criteria, but that doesn't generally happen a lot.

The subconscious criteria are based on many factors that are related to your past experiences. Therefore, you may fall in love with someone just because of your unresolved complexes, not because you genuinely love that person.

Actually, during most breakups people suffer great distress thinking that they had genuinely loved their ex-partners, while in reality they were just in need of anyone who would meet their criteria.

Looking at the above story, the heroine had felt financially insecure and was therefore searching for someone to compensate for her financial restrictions. This means that if she could find an alternative way to become wealthy, she might not have become attracted to that well-to-do person at all. This also means that you can feel devastated after a breakup because of issues related to your past, not because you were genuinely in love with the person who broke up with you.

It is important that you make time to think of all your criteria. Ask yourself, "What would I like, admire and need in my romantic partner?" Writing down your criteria will help you get to know yourself better. Therefore, you should take a piece of paper and pen and start writing down all the qualities that you would need in your partner.

Understanding our needs gives us a clear view of why we might become attached to certain people. Further on, I will be discussing the step you should take after you pinpoint your needs.

You would be amazed to see the same person receiving conflicting judgments of his character from different people.

That person might seem attractive and breathtaking to some people, whereas others might find them ordinary and unimpressive. In the psychology of "How to Make Someone Fall in Love with You" I discuss how there are specific traits that grab people's attention, while others are repulsive for most of those who meet them.

But mind you, I am saying 'most'; if you have these commonly desirable traits but you don't fulfill someone's criteria, he/she may not fall for you. So, if someone doesn't fall in love with you, it doesn't mean you are unattractive; it is because of his/her unconscious criteria.

Is It Love or Is It My Ego?

One thing that is very common about falling in love is that sometimes people confuse being in love with wanting to protect their egos and public image. How would it feel if people knew that you'd been abandoned by your partner? Or how would it feel if people knew that you couldn't satisfy your partner?

How many people do you know or have heard about that have unhappy relationships or marriages, but do not make any attempt to remedy their situation only because they are worried about what people will think of them?

In many cases, the couple's family and friends keep telling them that they are a match made in heaven. This kind of pressure makes it very hard for the couple to make the decision to split up. They try to ignore the things that are upsetting them about their relationship in order to live up to the social image that their community has of them. The end result is that they lead a discontented life.

Since we are a highly social species that depends on the approval of the social pack for our happiness and survival, it is natural that an intensely undesirable emotion arises in us when we break from the guidelines of the pack or disappoint others. Nevertheless, you should be careful not to let that be the cause of an even more undesirable feeling of depression.

Striving to live up to people's expectations may make you miserable. Dealing with disappointed people is like facing any other fear. Remember that we tend to exaggerate even though what we fear may not be as monstrous as we perceive it in our minds. The key to solving that problem is planning.

Be prepared to deal with people's surprise or disappointment on hearing the news of your breakup and to answer their questions diplomatically. The awkwardness of these situations is more manageable than continuing to live in misery. Remember that the longer you keep a failed relationship going, the more you expose yourself to pain and psychological harm.

One of the strongest reasons behind someone's distress after a breakup is the "involvement of the ego," which can make people feel depressed owing to their hurt ego, not their love for their ex-partners!

Take 20 seconds to reflect on this: Most of the psychological pain you endure when you are dealing with a breakup is, in truth, associated with the pain that your ego is suffering, not with your sadness over losing your partner. Knowing this is a turning point for many people who want to deal with rejection or a breakup.

Ask yourself this, "Does it *truly* have to do with the person I lost rather than with my hurt ego and wounded pride?"

Here are some of the most common thoughts that come to our minds after a breakup:

- What will people say when they know that I was jilted?
- Will they think less of me when they know?
- How will I face all the people who predicted the relationship would fail?
- How will I face people who told me that I wasn't good enough for my ex-partner?

You would suffer great distress as these thoughts can take control as soon as you are jilted. If you were living alone in the desert just with the person who broke up with you, you wouldn't get so depressed as you wouldn't have to worry about people's reactions to the news of the breakup.

Almost all people, though with varying degrees, care about their social image as seen by others. One of the most common misconceptions is that the person who is jilted is not good or worthy enough. It is this false belief that makes some people become depressed after a breakup.

If one ties his/her self-worth to something, the threat of losing that thing would be analogous to the threat of losing his/her self-worth. When people tie their self-worth to being accepted by their partners, they become more attached to their partners because a breakup would mean the loss of their self-worth.

People who go through a breakup become dispirited or depressed thinking, that their "soul mate" has broken up with them and that they will never be able to find someone as perfect as him/her, but the real reason might be their fear of facing people after their sense of self-worth has been shattered.

So, the very important question you should be asking yourself after breaking up with someone is, "Am I devastated because I've lost him/her or is it just the sting of my wounded ego?" Being the kind of human beings that we are, ego involvement plays a big part in causing the negative feelings we experience after a breakup. The feelings of love we have been harboring towards our ex-partners are, therefore, not the sole reason for our heartbreak.

I am not saying that the only cause of being in low spirits after a breakup is involvement of the ego, but it's one of the reasons that contribute to being downcast. As you read further in the book, you will be introduced to more reasons that can make someone become depressed after a breakup; the more reasons you understand and try to redress, the easier the breakup will be.

How Do You Get Over the Involvement of Your Ego?

There are two ways that can help you get over the involvement of the ego: build your self-confidence and be prepared to deal with people's reactions to the news of your breakup with your partner.

Telling everybody about the breakup as soon as it happens may seem like a rough blow to your ego, but it certainly has the effect of eliminating your feelings of wounded pride as this way will rid you of them quickly. You may dread ripping off a bandage quickly because you know it hurts, but you also know that it's better than tearing it off slowly. Once you tell people, you will experience a great relief, diametrically opposite to the mortification you'll continue to feel if you don't tell them.
Telling people can involve:

- Announcing to everyone, including your mutual friends that your relationship is over.
- Providing people who always thought that you were a match made in heaven with a good reason for the breakup in order to check their disappointment.

If you are now thinking of something like "But who cares about people's opinion? And why would I tell them anything when I just don't care what they think?" you may not be in need of this chapter, so skip to the next one.

As for building self-confidence, this will allow you to realize that going through a breakup doesn't mean that you are worthless, but rather it shows that there was some kind of incompatibility between you and your partner. Self-confidence will also allow you to ignore people's opinions, including those who thought they could foresee the failure of the relationship.

In addition to the abovementioned aspects, a lack of self-confidence has been found to be one of the main reasons for being depressed after a breakup. So, by developing your self-confidence, breakups will become much easier to deal with, as you will see in the coming pages.

Building self-confidence is a lengthy process, but you could speed it up by reading the condensed self-confidence articles found in www.2knowmyself.com. The articles found there contain tons of information that is straightforward, taking up a few pages instead of hundreds.

I will mention here one of the most important factors that contribute to developing self-confidence and which will help greatly in overcoming the involvement of your ego.

As we grow up and face different challenges and experiences and hear the stories of other people, we create our own belief system. The problem is that many of our beliefs may not be true and can damage our self-esteem and thwart our attempts at success in the different areas of our lives. Some examples of these false beliefs could be, "I can never develop myself," "I am no good," or "Everything I do is wrong." Unfortunately, if you give free reign to these erroneous assumptions, they will become self-destructive and stop you from achieving your potential. Everyone has the ability to do or become what they really want if only they believe they can do it. Our beliefs affect the way we act.

Monitor yourself speaking most of the time and you will realize that every time you feel you can't do something, there is a false belief behind your feeling that diminishes your will power. Reflect on this belief and try to analyze how you can achieve your aim. If you think, read and persevere, you will always find effective ways of doing it.

The same method can be applied to facing people when you are dealing with a breakup. Think of what you are worried about and try to see how serious you are making the matter seem in comparison with its actual magnitude, then logically analyze the situation and try to see how manageable the problem is. Only then will you be able to face it.

Love, Hatred and Emotions

Have you ever heard someone complain about his/her job?
Do you think that this person hates what they do at their job?
No they don't; they just hate the feelings they experience while doing their job.
Whenever you hate something it's because of the feelings you experience while doing it, not because of the thing itself.

One of my relatives always used to tell me that she hated having a prearranged schedule for meetings. Whenever she had a meeting she would feel tense until she arrived. What was actually happening was that she was having problems managing her stress. Since having a meeting on a prearranged date was always translated by her mind into stress, she disliked having those meetings. She didn't hate the idea of setting a schedule; she merely hated the feelings associated with it.

So what does this have to do with love? Love follows the same rule. You may be in love with the emotions you experience when you see someone rather than with the person himself/herself. That is, if you meet someone who makes you feel happy, by cracking jokes for example, you will inevitably start to like being around him/her. You will think you love this person, while you only love the emotions he/she induces in you.

Of course, what determines whether this person becomes a potential partner or only a best friend is down to your subconscious criteria. You may feel good whenever this person is around, but if he/she doesn't meet your criteria, he/she will probably be restricted to the friend zone.

The more intense the emotions you evoke in another person, the stronger their attachment will be to you. That is why meeting someone by coincidence in an exciting situation may result in your becoming attached to him/her. As you would then be feeling jubilant, you would mistakenly think that those feelings of excitement were caused in you by the person, not the situation.

This brings our attention to a very pivotal idea. You may think that you love a person and that you can't live without him/her, while the truth is you are just addicted to the feelings you experience when you are with him/her.

This means that if you could experience the same feelings with someone else you will forget about your ex-partner! Craving certain feelings means that you are emotionally starved, not that you miss your ex-partner!

When you feel that you miss someone, ask yourself the following question; "Do I miss him/her because I love him/her, or is it just that I miss the emotions I used to feel while he/she was around?"

And if "emotions" was the answer, you should ask yourself another question, "Can someone else fill the gap by arousing the same emotions in me?" Of course the answer is "yes"; your subconscious mind merely misses the emotions, not the person himself/herself.

A very good, although a slightly extreme example of this which many people experience is how one might fall in love a lot, ending one relationship only to start another one. Of course people who fall in love frequently are not the only ones who experience attraction to emotions rather than people. Many people can experience this without realizing what they are going through.

But if we think about it, we will be able to work out that the common denominator in the multiple relationships of a certain person is the emotions that he/she experiences while being with their different partners. However, if you ask that person, he/she will tell you that on every occasion they'd been in love with their partner, regardless of the emotions they experienced.

Remember that you should answer this next question rationally, not emotionally: "Is it truly about missing this person or is mostly about missing the way I felt when I was in the relationship?"

This doesn't mean that you weren't in love with your partner, or that you were emotionally unfaithful to him/her. Being emotionally unfaithful involves allowing your passing fantasies about other people to diminish your love for your partner. But could it be that much of our happiness in any relationship is based on our experiencing certain feelings? The answer is, "Yes. On many occasions that's the case."

Where Have I Seen You Before?

Our subconscious mind thinks in a very simplistic way; it believes that people who look alike have similar personalities and behaviors. Suppose you meet someone who becomes a wonderful friend of yours, then you meet another person who looks just that friend, your subconscious mind will most likely think that the other person will be kind and friendly as well.

That is to say, you will find yourself getting a good first impression of certain people just because they look like old friends. The subconscious mind tends to associate people's looks with their behavior, and that's why you form a first impression of people the moment you see them.

Now, what if you meet a person who looks like someone you really loved and admired previously, but with whom your relationship has ended? What will certainly happen is that you will like this person and you may even eventually fall in love with him/her. Some people fall in love with certain people just because they look like their ex-partners. The funny part is that most of these people never realize it unless someone points it out to them.

Sometimes, you may become attached to someone just because they resemble an old friend or someone you have been in love with before. Although you think that you are deeply in love with that person because he/she is cheerful, handsome, kind, and so on, the truth is that you are attracted to him/her because of the association your subconscious mind is making.

I know a lot of folk who fall in love with certain people because they resemble others who influenced their lives before. A good example of this is the attachment to those people who look like your parents. It has been found that girls are attracted to men who look like their fathers, provided they were on good terms with them. The same happens to men; they are attracted to women who look like their mothers if they have a good relationship with them.

This doesn't stop at fathers and mothers, but it also happens with other relatives who influenced your life in a positive way, be it a sister or an uncle. The subconscious mind craves finding someone who is similar to a person you feel comfortable around.

Do you know what all this means?
You may be in a love with a person just because they look like someone you have been in love with before! You should also know that you may be having problems forgetting about that person because you think that he/she is "the one."

I know a girl who almost always fell in love with and admired guys who were overweight. She told me that many people asked her why she was so attracted to them specifically. For a long time, she didn't know why, but she explained that she felt they were kinder than other people. Lately she has reflected on the reason and realized that the kindest person she ever dealt with in her life was her grandmother, who was generous, warm-hearted and most importantly, extremely obese. Ever since she was a young girl, she was the apple of her grandmother's eye.

Her grandmother was always the one who cared for her and made her wishes come true. That is why her mind associates obesity with kindness.

Therefore, you should realize that this person you are now in love with may be a counterpart of another person. Do you still think that you are genuinely in love with that person now?

This is also one of the things that gives a good explanation of the phenomenon of falling in love at first sight; as soon as you see a person who looks like someone you were attached to in the past, you automatically become attached to this person.

By the way, this is not limited to physical appearance; you could fall in love with someone because he/she walks or talks in the same way as the person you were once attached to. Again, you should ask yourself, "Am I really in love with that person? Or am I just seeing in the relationship a reflection of my past experiences?"

One problem that often arises from the way in which the subconscious mind works is that the associations it makes are sometimes faulty. For example, you might meet a girl who looks just like your mother when she is young and fall in love with her, but eventually discover that her personality is a lot different from your mother's. This indicates how illogical it is to remain attached to someone merely because they resemble someone you used to cherish.

A good question you may be asking yourself at this stage is, "Will I be able to realize when I'm attracted to someone just because he/she resembles someone I love? Do I need a personal coach to help me develop a keen eye for it?"

The answer to the first question is "yes"; you can definitely find this out by thinking about it.
Ask yourself, "Is this relevant to my case?" and "Is there a certain aspect of his/her physical appearance, way of speaking or movement similar to that of someone I once loved or admired?"

In answer to the second question, you don't really need a coach for this because if you can somehow relate what you've read to your life, you only need to reflect on it. You'll be surprised to find how much you can find out yourself just by making the time to think about it.

Lack of Intimate Relationships

We are all born with a strong need for intimacy and a sense of belonging. If this need is left ungratified, it will inevitably produce feelings of emptiness and depression. You might be thinking that the more people you know, the more you will satisfy your need for intimacy, but this is an totally erroneous belief.

Even if you have hundreds of friends, you will still feel lonely if your relationship with them isn't intimate. If you want to get over a feeling of loneliness, you have to become intimate with someone, even if the people you can be intimate with are very few in comparison to the number of people you know. This will give you the satisfaction of belonging to a group of people who sincerely care about you.

Intimacy is not related to the number of people you know, but to the quality of the relationships you have with them. Having a meaningful, intimate relationship with two of your friends is much better than having superficial relationships with hundreds of people.

Since intimacy is the absence of loneliness, feeling lonely is a signal your brain is sending you to tell you that you have an intimacy problem. Everyone who feels lonely needs to build a few intimate relationships to get rid of that feeling.

An intimate relationship can be defined as a relationship where both partners communicate openly and frankly, telling each other their deepest fears, worries and interests.

The reason for someone having a non-intimate relationship with a close friend is the fear of being exposed, which stems from the fear of disapproval. Some people might fear sharing everything about themselves so that they won't disappoint their friends who disapprove their actions.

The question now is, "What does this have to do with getting over someone?" There is a very strong connection between a lack of intimacy and failing to get over someone, as sometimes people start a relationship to compensate for their lack of intimacy with others. This happens when:

- Someone doesn't have intimate friends. Therefore, he/she starts a relationship in order to have an intimate partner instead.
- Someone has many superficial relationships rather than intimate ones.
- Someone feels lonely and longs for a relationship just to get rid of their feeling of loneliness.
- Someone feels neglected by his/her friends.

People sometimes start relationships to compensate for one of the above problems, but of course their subconscious minds never allow them to realize that they are seeking a relationship solely to escape from certain troubles. Instead, they make them think that they are deeply in love with their partners.

Falling in love in order to conquer loneliness can make some people become strongly attached to their partners. Ending the relationship therefore becomes a fear they don't want to face.

They may even choose to ignore problems with their partners and leave them unsolved in order to prevent conflict from ending their relationships. If you are in a similar situation, you should bear in mind that you are afraid of being lonely, not of losing your partner per se.

Some relationships are only a product of people feeling an urge to satisfy their need for intimacy. In that case, even if the relationship doesn't satisfy a lonely person's need for intimacy, he/she won't think of ending it in the hope that, one day, it will satisfy his/her needs.

As you will probably infer from all this, the subconscious mind always buries the real reasons behind your behavior. The result is an attachment to someone while thinking that he/she is "the one" or your irreplaceable "soul mate." You should remember that there is no such thing as a soul mate; there are, however, unmet needs that goad you into starting relationships that you think will save you from being lonely.

If you realize that you can't deal with your breakup because you feel lonely, you should fix your relationship with your friends. If you can become intimate with some of them, you will find that you are no longer attached to your ex-partner. The only reason you were attached to that person in the first place is that your subconscious mind was craving intimacy; as soon as you provide yourself with another source of intimacy, you will no longer need that partner.

At this stage people usually ask, "Well, I simply don't have any close friendships. What do I do now?"
This is exactly the right question at the right time.

There are two ways of building close friendships. The first one is to take a close look at your circle of friends. Are there any trustworthy people you can start to develop a close bond with? Can you start working on your relationship with these people so that your shallow conversations will, over time, become more intimate, meaningful ones?

If you think this is impossible, you should try the second solution. Get to know new people and widen your circle of acquaintances by participating in different activities. The more people you know, the bigger your chance will be of meeting someone you can build an intimate relationship with. Take up a sport, join a book club, enrol on a training course in something that interest you, or join a charity organization. You are bound to meet one or two people taking part in these activities who you would want to become intimate with.

If you realize that one of the main reasons you are attached to your partner is your need for intimacy, you need to know that it is very crucial that you start taking action to remedy this situation.

Many of the people I have coached have raised objections against developing new intimate relationships, but most, if not all of them, were able to find people they could bond with after trying out the "new activities solution." if you hold onto the belief that these solutions are impractical without first trying them, you will be restricting yourself and wasting an opportunity to recover from your breakup.

What Are You Trying To Prove?

Suppose that a man failed to establish good relationships with his classmates when he was a child. The subconscious mind of this person never forgets this failure and it desperately tries to set the situation right. But since the child has already grown up, his subconscious mind tries to compensate for his earlier problem by making the grown-up man eager to establish good relationships with everyone around him.

Some people have a mysterious need to make other people fall in love with them and also for getting to know new people. These people are trying to change their pasts by taking control of their present situation.

The subconscious mind recalls the old situation every time they start a new relationship and tries to do what it failed to do in the past, namely being agreeable and friendly towards others. That's why the addiction to making new friends or making people fall in love with them never seems to end, or until they prove to themselves that they have succeeded in doing what they failed to do in the past.

The question you should ask yourself if you are a relationship addict is: "What are you trying to prove to yourself? Is your past haunting you and making you get into relationships only to do what you failed to do earlier on in your life?"

The following examples will illustrate how some people try to convince themselves that they can do something they failed to do in the past:

- A person who has always had impaired leadership skills will try to become a leader among his friends.
- A person who was ignored and dismissed when he/she was a child will want to be loved by everyone and be the center of attention.
- A man who failed to get on with girls with a certain belief system or from a particular cultural background will always try to date these kinds of girl.

The examples that can be given are numerous, but the concept will always remain the same. Whenever people fail to do something in their past, their subconscious minds always try to force them to succeed in accomplishing it later on in their lives. That's why some people become addicted to having certain types of relationship since it's their only way to change their past.

I will try to give an example to illustrate what I mean, but be careful not to think that this is the only example there is. Use it only as an illustration of the idea.
Suppose that a man in his early years wasn't very popular with his classmates.

People didn't include him in their games or invite him to their birthday parties. During his teenage years, most of the pretty girls avoided him or maybe didn't even notice him most of the time. He felt that no one wanted to be his friend and was badly hurt when his popular classmates made fun of him.

Growing up, he tried learning more about how to deal with people and make friends, but no matter how many friends he made, he still felt he was the same unpopular boy he was back when he was in school. One day he met one of the popular girls he used to see at his sports practice when he was a young man and who he had secretly admired. Although she couldn't remember him, it became obvious that she now found him a very interesting fellow.

He managed to impress her and they eventually got into a relationship together. Although he sincerely liked her, the main reason he started a relationship with her was to prove to himself that he was good enough to be with a popular person.

So, if you can relate to this anecdote you should be able to deduce that even though you might have liked certain things about your partner, were you still trying to prove something to yourself?

That's also why lots of people lose interest in a relationship as soon as they realize that their partners love them as they didn't get into the relationship because they genuinely loved their partners, but because of their need to change their pasts.

After being jilted you should ask yourself an important question, "Was I trying to prove something to myself by getting into this relationship? Was I trying to change my past through this relationship?"

If your answers were "yes," you should know that you weren't in love with nor even liked your ex-partner; he/she was only a priceless tool which you could use to change your past. Every single day, millions of people fall in love because of the desire of their subconscious minds to help them get over the past failures that were haunting them.

He Is Everything To Me!

"He is everything to me. I can't imagine my life without him. Life is impossible without him."

Why do people sometimes think it impossible to live without a certain person? And why can someone become everything to someone else?

Some people who have unhealthy relationships tend to ignore their own interests, needs, friends, hobbies and passions solely for the sake of being with the person they love. These people gradually take the following actions after getting into a relationship:

- They stop seeing their close friends.
- They stop contacting their friends regularly. Both this action and the previous one close the doors to intimacy with their friends, thus making them totally dependent on their partners to satisfy that need. In other words, their partners become the only people who can provide them with emotional well-being.
- They stop practicing their favorite hobbies. This makes life become boring and creates a need for something that relieves this boredom, which they mistakenly believe to be the relationship itself.
- They compromise their own goals and plans when they think that this is the price they need to pay to stay with their partners. This makes a person's life meaningless unless they are in that relationship.

Clearly, these actions slowly change the person from being their normal self to someone who is completely dependent on his/her partner. When you sacrifice everything for the sake of one person, your life will undoubtedly become intolerable if that person decides to end the relationship.

How many times have you seen people who are in the habit of keeping very busy and having far-reaching plans suddenly give up everything after getting into a relationship? Making your partner the center of your life is one thing, but shutting down your life is another entirely. Making time to be with your partner is certainly crucial, but going on with your life is equally important.

If you give up your plans and prospects for someone, your relationship with him/her will soon go from being healthy to being dependent and needy. Moreover, the day it dawns on you that you have lost many people and opportunities, you will become severely depressed. Remember that giving up your identity, the people you know and the things you love in order to build your relationship with your partner will not turn out to be for his/her benefit or yours in the long run.

If you are in an unhealthy relationship, you have most likely made your relationship "everything," and that's why you feel like you have lost everything when the relationship ends.

If this is what has happened to you, instead of crying over your ex-partner, it's time you got back to your goals, plans and favorite hobbies.

Call your friends to get your social life back on track. A few weeks later you will discover that you don't need your partner because your life won't have to revolve around him/her anymore.

You will be surprised to see how relieved and tranquil you feel as soon as you start working on getting your life back. Instead of desperately begging someone to take you back so that you can be happy again, I advise you to get up now and start planning how you can get your former life back. This is a major step that will work like magic as soon as you start following it.

The next time you get into a relationship, make sure that you never give up any of the things that are important to you. You should remember that healthy relationships are those in which partners live their respective lives individually, but share their happy and sad moments as if they were one person.

Below are some tips you can make use of the next time you get into a relationship:

- Even if your friends like your new partner, you must make time regularly to meet with them alone. You might be happy that the people who are dear to you like each other, but you must not forget that your friends will want to spend time with you alone. This will also give your partner the chance to have some quality time with his/her friends, thus sparing you the trouble of being blamed by your partner's friends for taking him/her away from them.

- It is endearing to want to spend most of your free time with the person you love, but you should also make plans to keep doing the things you like and that are important to you. Giving up everything for your partner will sooner or later negatively affect your relationship. It's appealing to get caught up in a new romance, to meet the parents of your partner, and to have a great time with him/her. It sounds perfect, doesn't it? However, there are very important things that you may be leaving behind on the dock while your love boat sets sail. Don't forget about your own life, because it matters; nothing is worth losing it over.

- If your partner is possessive and does not want you to care about anything except your relationship together, you have to remember that if you comply with his/her wishes, you will face a big problem later on. Don't fight with your partner when you think his/her demands are unreasonable, but keep explaining to him/her that you can't quit doing the things that are important to you until he/she can adapt to your lifestyle. There are two things you should keep in mind: firstly, don't impose your beliefs on your partner or fight with him/her when you have different opinions because this will create tensions rather than make your partner more understanding. Secondly, you should give your partner a lot of time to develop a close, intimate relationship with you.

There Is Just Too Much That Time Cannot Erase

In any relationship people usually associate their happy memories with the person they have been in love with, thinking that their partner was behind the positive feelings they experienced. When a relationship lasts for a long time then ends in a breakup, people usually have a hard time trying to forget all the good memories they experienced with his/her partner. This is one of the reasons people might fail to get over a partner.

When your subconscious mind gets used to harboring certain good experiences and memories, it tends to become attached to them in such a way that their absence creates a sensation of craving. This is what happens to almost everyone; a person craves the memories while actually thinking that he/she is missing their partner.

This means that if you find someone else who can provide you with the same good feelings by sharing the same happy memories with you, you won't need your ex-partner, who you thought you wanted to get back together with!

You are attached to the good times you had together along with the nice places you went to with this ex-partner. People always confuse their happy memories with their ex-partner and think that they can't over him/her, while really they are only nostalgic for the memories.

This is the same reason why you forget about your old relationships as soon as you get into a new good one; when you find another source of good memories and feelings, you forget the old memories, and with them your ex-partner.

You might be telling yourself, "But I sometimes go into a new relationship and I keep comparing my new partner to the old one until the old one wins." This only happens when you rush into a relationship specifically to forget about the old one, without actually having any genuine loving emotions for your new partner.

After a breakup you should ask yourself this question: "Do I really miss my ex-partner, or am I just craving the good memories?" If you realize that you need the memories more than the person, you should also realize that you can create new memories with someone else, provided that he/she meets your subconscious criteria."

In my other book "How to Make Someone Fall in Love with you," this concept is one of the techniques used to help you keep your partner attached to you. By creating lasting memories with a person, you make sure he/she will find it difficult to stay away from you.

What I truly advise you to do here is to use the "block" method. Every time your brain recalls one of your happy memories with your ex-partner, you have to *block* it. That is to say, you should instantly ban yourself from pursuing the thought since you are the one in control of your own thoughts.

Every time you have a thought, you should say, "*block.*" Remember that your mind will fight you and try to present you with more thoughts, in which case you should say, "*Block, block, and block.*" After a while, your mind will relent and stop bringing up those thoughts. Don't allow a single one of those undesirable thoughts to pass unblocked because every single time you block a thought, you are gaining an advantage in the fight against your mind. You should be able to take control of whatever thoughts your mind comes up with in no time.

"Awe, I remember how she used to look at me, it was just breathtaking-" *Block!*
"Gosh, this tenderness-" *Block!*
"I was important to him, you know-" *Block!*
"I'll never forget that day-" *Block!*
"He was there for me when I needed him-" *Block again!*
"No one will ever love me the same way-" *Block!*

Blocking all these memories will gradually diminish the ability of your mind to recall them, which will go a long way to helping you get over your ex-partner.

Many people succeed in doing this for some time, but then they give in to their thoughts. This is either because something happens that reminds them of their ex-partners, or simply because they are overwhelmed with depression and they decide to give up. Consistency is the key to succeeding in blocking memories. It takes a little self-discipline, but is certainly achievable.

When coaching people to do this, I often notice how some people deviate at some point. Is it possible that you will make the same mistake? Yes, it's definitely possible. However, once you realize you are making that mistake, you should get back on track. Once you're back on it, you will reach the finish-line in no time.

So what is it that you should do? *Block, block, and block.* And that's it.

Everything Reminds Me of Him/Her

Many people tend to keep reminiscing about their ex-partners long after their relationships have ended. This usually happens because of the associations that their minds have formed between their ex-partners and different things. For example:

- Visiting certain places frequently with your partner will result in associating him/her with those places.
- Listening to certain songs while you were in love with your partner will make you associate your relationship with those songs.
- The topics you used to talk about with your partner will become associated in your mind with him/her.
- You will also associate everything you used to do with your partner with him/her.

Therefore, anything that can spark any of these associations will remind you of your ex-partner. You might be asking yourself, "How are these associations formed?"

When two events keep recurring at the same time, the mind starts to associate them in such a way that you remember one whenever the other occurs. This is called classical conditioning and it's a well-known concept.

Now the question is, how can you get rid of this conditioning if you don't want your ex-partner to remain on your mind? The good news is that if the first event keeps happening without any recurrence of the second one, the events soon become disassociated from each other in your mind. For example, if after your breakup you keep visiting the same places alone that you used to go to with your partner, after some time you won't remember your partner every time you visit that place.

But you might say, "I do this already, but I can't forget about my ex-partner; the association sometimes becomes even stronger when I keep visiting the same places we used to go to together." This is completely normal and only happens because you keep thinking about your ex-partner while you are in those places.

For example, if you used to sit by the sea together, thinking about him/her while you are sitting there will only make the association stronger. What you should do is to sit by the sea and deliberately think about something else. I know that every now and then a passing thought will come into your mind, but you can always dismiss it and think about something else.

What most people do is that they go to the same places and start daydreaming about their ex-partner. They start imagining how a conversation with their ex-partner would go if they were trying to work it out and get back together. Other people try to avoid going to the places or doing the things that remind them of their ex-partners, which is also totally wrong. These people are doing nothing except ignoring the problem, which will remain unsolved until they take action. The right thing do is to live your life normally and go to all the places you used to go with your ex-partner, while not thinking about him/her at all. Even if thoughts of him/her come to mind, you should be able to control them.

Again, let's have a look at an example to demonstrate what I mean. If you pass by or sit in a cafe where you used to spend time with your ex-partner, you will start to notice and relate many things, maybe silly things, to some of your memories together.

You might notice the menu and remember a time when you discussed how you both hated coffee, or you might notice the table you used to sit at and remember a certain conversation of yours that you still cherish, or you might even see a waiter who used to serve you and remember a nice compliment he once gave both of you.

Allowing all these memories to flash before your eyes won't help you if you *really* want to get over your ex-partner. You know what you have to do by now, don't you?
Block the train of these thoughts. Every time you have a thought that makes your heart ache for your lost partner, you should right away say, *"Block!"*

Another thing that has proved helpful, and which I will discuss in more detail later on, is listening to songs. You should stop listening to sad songs and relating to them. You might even find that easier to do than blocking.

Don't let those sweet memories and thoughts control you.
Most people fall prey to the spell of those memories, which is why most people fail to get over their ex-partner quickly.
But if you are determined to get over your ex-partner, you will easily be able to *block* those thoughts.

But I Still See Him/Her Around

What if you were in a relationship with someone who works with you? Or what if they are studying with you at the same college? Won't that make getting over him/her harder to achieve?

No, it won't. The more you see the person without thinking of him/her as a potential partner, the easier your mind will conceive that your ex-partner is now no more than a friend. People usually have a hard time getting over people they see on a daily basis because they do the following:

- Whenever they see them, they start to think about the possibility of their getting back together.
- Whenever they are alone, they start thinking about their ex-partner.
- They sometimes daydream while watching their ex-partner.
- They try to avoid their ex-partner, which makes the problem worse.

The correct thing to do to deal with your ex-partner is not to ignore him/her, but to deal with him/her as you would deal with a friend. Ignoring your ex-partner will only result in putting off the problem, not solving it.

Even supposing you are agonizingly hurt following your breakup, you should greet you ex-partner, even if in a curt manner, if you happen to see him/her. If getting over your partner has the added difficulty of seeing him/her every day, it is advisable that you choose to communicate with him/her, even if very briefly.

Your subconscious mind will help you let go of your ex-partner only if you give it proof that everything has come to an end between you. The absence of this proof is what can stop you from thinking about your ex-partner and dealing with him/her normally, as you would deal with any acquaintance.

Sometimes the problem is not simply seeing your ex-partner, but seeing him/her with his/her new partner. In this case, you aren't in distress because you are still in love with your ex-partner, but because of the ego issues I talked about earlier.

If you are going through this, you should now understand that your heartache is not caused by the fact that you are still in love with your ex-partner, but by the pain that your ego is suffering. I know that these situations can be awkward and hurtful, but if they happen lots of times and if you don't think much of it, you will eventually get used to it and therefore feel no pain when you see them together.

I know a girl who said that she was perfectly happy about ending her relationship with her partner until she saw him with another girl. She then started comparing herself to his new partner, she felt lonely, and suddenly wanted to get back together with him. When she realized that her feelings came from her hurt ego rather than from her love for him, she stopped making those harmful comparisons, stopped checking their social networking pages, and decided to stop thinking about him and his new partner. The revelation that her wounded ego was controlling her thoughts helped her take control of her life and move on.

Some people try to get into a relationship immediately after a breakup in order to preserve their social status and show others that they are not broken or lonely. This is a big mistake, because if you decide to do this you might rashly choose any partner who happens to serve that purpose, which will eventually lead to another breakup and more emotional damage.

Act wisely and deal with the root cause of the problem. As you read on and from what you have already read, think of any instances you can relate to and start taking action. There is not a single person who has done this and failed to recover from his/her breakup. Knowing the reason is half the cure; taking action is the other half. If only you do both, you will always live happily.

But He's My Soul Mate!

"But he's my soul mate; I fell in love with him the moment I saw him. No one is as outgoing or kind as he is. He knows what to say and when to say it."

I am sure that you've heard these phrases many times, and you may have even said them yourself. Let's analyze these phrases together:

He/She's my soul mate: I believe that there is no such a thing as a soul mate, although I still don't have any proof to support my theory.

The soul mate concept is one of the biggest lies that the media has propagated over the years through movies, songs and poems. Yes, you may have found a wonderful person, but that doesn't mean that he/she is the most wonderful person in the world; you could still meet someone who is even better than him/her.

I fell in love with him/her the moment I saw him/her: This means I knew that he/she could fulfill my subconscious criteria the moment I saw him/her.

Love at first sight is nothing more than finding someone who you think matches your criteria at first sight. People who always fall in love at first sight usually have certain criteria that are essentially based on looks. That's why when they see a person for the first time, they can make out whether he/she fulfills their criteria or not. On the other hand, people who fall in love a few weeks or a few months after they meet a person usually have deeper and more sophisticated subconscious criteria.

You can also fall in love with someone at first sight simply because they look like someone you have loved before, or sometimes you don't even notice this fact and yet fall in love with that person for no apparent reason.

Suppose you are a man who is on good terms with his mother. If you meet a girl who has similar facial features to your mother, your subconscious mind will be quick to detect the physical resemblance, even if your conscious mind does not notice it. In this case, your subconscious mind will think that being intimate with this person who looks like your mother will make you happy, just like your relationship with your mother used to make you happy.

This could also happen if you break up with a girl that you have been in love with and then you meet a girl who looks exactly like her a few years later. Again, consciously you may not notice that they look alike, but your subconscious mind will not fail to notice the similarity and the result will be falling in love with her.

We can conclude that one of the reasons we fall in love is the desire of the subconscious mind to bring you close to people who can make you happy. However, this is not the only reason; you can even fall in love at first sight with someone because they walk or talk in the same way as someone you have been in love with before, or whom you admire.

This means that the person you call your "soul mate" or "the one" is only the counterpart of someone whom you have met before and who has influenced your life in a positive way. This fact alone undermines the concept of "the one," because if you meet someone else who also fulfills your criteria, you will fall in love with him/her as well.

What if your so-called soul mate fulfills 45% of your criteria? Doesn't that mean if you meet someone else who fulfills 50% of your criteria, you will fall in love with him/her?

This person you think is your soul mate is actually someone who could meet most of your criteria. But that doesn't tell you that you can't meet someone who can fulfill more of your criteria!

Don't cry over someone who ticks 45 boxes on your list; instead contemplate the fact that the world is big enough to contain people who can tick 50, 55 or 60 of those boxes, and that we are destined to fall in love with the person who meets most of these criteria.

A friend of mine went through an experience we can all relate to, and she asked me to share it in this book to help other people see what she had failed to see before them.

She was once introduced to a friend of a friend to help him out with certain projects that he was working on. Because she was very busy at that time, she tried to put off their meeting, but she wasn't able to. She later realized that it would have been a great misfortune if she hadn't met him.

After a few days of working with him, she started realizing how wonderful this man was. They had a lovely time working together and she knew that she had never admired a man as much as she admired him. She began to think that he was her soul mate and that having met him, she would never fall in love or be attracted to anyone else ever again.

She confessed her love to him saying, "I've met so many men in my life. Out of all the places that I've ever been to and all the men that I've gotten to know, I've never liked a guy the way I like you."

"No man has ever taken up all of my attention, made my jaw drop, or drawn me towards him like you do. All of these are understatements; words can't express how I feel."

"I look at you when you're speaking and I wonder how there could ever be someone who is so witty and intelligent."

She also said to him, "I told a friend at work, who looked at me in disbelief when I told her that I've completely lost interest in all other men. Since there's no one like you in the whole world, no other man would ever attract or interest me. I've never wanted to be with anyone the way I want to be with you."

To cut a long story short, their relationship had to end.
Now that she's over it, she says that she still knows very well the things that attracted her to him and she still believes that he's one of the most wonderful people that she has ever met, but she also now knows that she can definitely meet someone else who would be equally or even more wonderful.

It was a relief for her to notice this, and it's important that you notice this yourself. Yes, your ex-partner might have had an outstanding character, but he/she is not the only wonderful person in the world.

That's why you might meet and fall in love with someone while you are already in a relationship. Another question you should ask yourself is, how many soul mates or people that you could call "the one" have you met before?

If it's your first experience of love, you will certainly think your partner is "the one," but if it's your third or fourth relationship, you must have noticed that you've had many soul mates throughout your life.

No one is as outgoing as him/her: Up until now, I haven't met anyone more outgoing than my partner.

If you haven't met anyone who is as outgoing as him/her, that doesn't mean there aren't hundreds of other outgoing people you haven't met yet. The world is full of outgoing people, and so meeting one of them doesn't tell you that you've met them all; it only tells you that you haven't met more cheerful people yet.

We all like to be around people who make us feel good and this is one very distinct thing that outgoing people certainly do. Yes, I realize how wonderful your relationship with your ex-partner must have been, but you also need to realize that you have a big chance of meeting people who are more outgoing.

He/She knows what to say and the right time to say it: one of my subconscious criteria was "A person who knows how to express himself/herself well." He/she meets this criterion perfectly.

A person might meet one of your criteria but again, does this mean that he is the only one in the world who can meet it? We are talking about only one criterion here; do you know what the possibility of meeting someone else who has the same capacity for meeting that criterion is? It's certainly a great possibility. There is no such thing as "the one" or a "soul mate"; there are only certain people who meet some of your criteria and so make you think that they are one of a kind.

To put it simply, there *are* plenty of other amazing fish in the sea for you.

The Media & Everyday Crime

The media, with its romantic movies and love songs, is one of the strongest forces affecting the health of your future relationships. So many songs and movies that have become popular are the product of a market of false hopes about how you can fall in love with someone who doesn't live up to your notion of the perfect partner just because love can change the way you think.

This leads to one of two things; either you feel a lack of satisfaction in your current relationship because it's not as romantic as those you see in the movies, or you stay single for a long while and wait for your so-called "soul mate," hoping that he/she will bring you the "ever after" happiness.

The human mind responds to the indoctrination caused by movies and songs in a manner that is beyond your imagination. Some teenagers commit crimes right after seeing violence committed in a movie, and some adults stay scared for weeks because of a horror movie that they happened to watch.

I still remember how a lot of strange accidents took place in Egypt a few years ago on the release of a particularly convincing action/ thriller movie. The movie affected the people who watched it and manipulated them in a way that was reflected in those accidents.

Returning to love, the type of romantic love that the media hypes up is very far from reality. The media presents love as the solution to all your problems and the road to ultimate happiness; it makes you think that all you have to do to overcome your problems and live happily is to find someone who truly loves you and to stick with him/her forever.

When someone starts a relationship with these expectations in mind, he/she always keeps comparing his/her partner to their "fairy tale" movie-like partners, and that's where problems arise. You start to feel that your partner is neither as romantic nor as perfect as he/she is supposed to be.

What's even worse is that you discover that your old problems are not solved by love! They have, on the contrary, increased after the birth of your first child or your first experience of financial difficulties.

Whatever you have seen in the media falls into one category: Toxic ideas that are far from being truthful. Real love starts with attraction, then passes through a phase of affection, an finally slowly turns into an intimate relationship.

The media committed an even worse crime when it started tackling the issue of breakups. It feeds our minds with ideas such as "I can never live without you," and "you are the one for me." Constant repetition turns these ideas into ardent, unconquerable beliefs, with the result that you feel devastated after a breakup and grief-stricken over losing what the media calls "the one."

If you always listen to songs that deliver messages such as "I'm broken because you are gone," or "life is meaningless without you," your attitude after a breakup will be a reflection of the songs you listen to. Imagine how a mere song can keep you from recovering from a breakup! That's because songs can brainwash people.

Listening to certain songs or watching specific movies is not harmful as long as you keep in mind that you are watching or listening to fiction which is perhaps somewhat exaggerated, and which you therefore cannot relate to.

If you are currently broken-hearted, you should stop listening to those songs or watching those movies immediately, because each time you listen to or watch them, the belief that you can't live without your ex-partner is nurtured in you, gradually making your recovery impossible.

How can you tell yourself that you will be strong and that you will forget him/her while you're listening to songs that install in your mind ideas such as, "I can't live without you," "don't leave me in this pain," or "give me a second chance"?

If you are determined to recover from your breakup, you should stop listening to those songs in order not to let the tree grow. If your distress is the seed, those songs and movies are the water supply that can turn it into a tree. Therefore, you should cut off the water supply before it's too late.

You'd be better off listening to songs with diametrically opposite ideas which convince you that you will be alright even if someone has broken up with you. Although these songs are rare, they certainly exist. Find them and replace your current playlist with a new, positive one in order to speed up your recovery from your breakup.

Positive Media

Let's say that the lyrics of a song start with:

Since you left me, everything's wrong

Without you here, I can't get along

My life is nothing without you

If you'll only give me a second chance

Or, for instance, if the lyrics of a song speak of romantically not giving up on the person who has given up on you just because your life would be ruined without him/her; what do you think that would do to you? Do you think this type of music affects you positively?

How many times does it happen that you listen to a song that fills you with negative energy as you go through a breakup or a failed relationship? How many times has the media taken advantage of you by fixating on the same advertisement or commercial that touches you in a negative way?

If the media has the ability to indoctrinate us through repetition, why not turn this into an advantage by listening to positive media that can help us recover faster? I'm not recommending a specific band or song because normally we have different tastes, but I do strongly recommend that you find your positive energy through songs that promote courage and movies that inspire optimism rather than pessimism.

Make sure that you have a playlist of songs with positive messages, especially right after breaking up with someone. Through repetition, your mind will start to take in the positive messages just like it did with the negative ones, and thus you'll recover faster.

Choosing to focus only on positive things in the media is not only important when it comes to breaking up, but it's also crucial to living a happy life. There are songs that can depress you, while others can lift your mood, and so being more careful about the choices you make will have a strong impact on your life.

In 1949, two neuroscientists discovered that we have something called the Reticular Activating System (or RAS) located in the brain stem. Perhaps the most important function of the RAS is to control consciousness. Other than controlling sleep and wakefulness, it gives you the ability to consciously focus your attention on something. This is the eye-opener that I will be discussing here.

Have you ever decided to buy a new car and suddenly you started seeing the make of car you intend to buy everywhere you go? In the streets, in magazine advertisements, in commercials and also parked up in parking lots?

This brand has always been there, but because you've activated your RAS, you began to *"see"* it. Because you've focused your attention on this specific brand, your brain has been tuned to spot it wherever it crops up.

Your RAS is the automatic mechanism inside your brain that brings all the information relevant to a certain item or topic to your attention. If you direct your attention to something, your brain will make you detect its presence.

If you focus on how weak you are at overcoming your heartbreak, this is exactly what will be proven to you. If you decide to shift your focus onto being strong, it will direct your attention to your capacity to do anything. The choice is yours; be your own positive media and help yourself with thoughts about your own strength to move your attention in the right direction.

From now on, decide to focus on blocking weak thoughts and direct your attention to powerful ones instead.

From Passionate Love to Compassionate Love

Most couples fail to understand that passionate love does not last more than three years. They never prepare themselves to move from passionate love to compassionate love with the result that their relationships collapse.

In order for the relationship to survive, a move from passionate to compassionate love is essential. You should be aware of the fact that passion can be a very good incentive for starting a relationship, but it can never sustain that relationship. At a certain point, mutual respect and intimacy must become more predominant. This transforms passion into affection, which will make the relationship become stronger as time passes.

Again, the media has played a role in brainwashing the minds of people in such a way that makes them believe that relationships can remain forever based on passion. A few years after couples get married, they start to notice that their passion is fading and because of the influence of the media, they start to think that the problem is with their incorrect choice of partner, and so they get divorced.

What they fail to understand is that they are moving into a new phase that is of more value and depth. If they are patient enough they will come to realize that this phase is more beautiful than the first phase of passion. However, this doesn't mean that they should abandon the first one.

Plan your future so that you won't get caught up in routine. Focus your attention on the relationship and you will be able to keep this passionate phase going as well. Whether you are able to retain the passionate phase or not, you should be able to understand that you have just started a new phase that is deeper and stronger. Learning that there are phases in a relationship, and keeping this fact in mind can help you better understand and maintain a healthy and meaningful relationship.

Don't grieve over the fact that your ex-partner only liked you at the beginning, but then began to get bored of you due to this shift in your relationship phase. Sometimes this false belief can make people feel that they are unlovable.

This thought can make you hang onto your pain, which is not related to the breakup itself, but to what it made you think about yourself. Erroneous as that idea is, it can damage your self-confidence and self-esteem.
Every relationship in the world passes from the passionate to the compassionate stage, which is the normal maturing of the relationship.

The first phase is characterized by devoted attention and excitement, but the second stage is more intimate. Now that you are aware of this, you can try to maintain both statuses during the maturity phase of your next relationship by trying to maintain the element of excitement. When your relationship undergoes the transformation from being passionate to being compassionate, you should know it's not because you are no longer interesting to your partner; it's the normal evolution of any relationship.

Compensation

One of the main reasons people fall in love is compensating for their early childhood experiences. A man who was always rejected by blond girls during his teenage years will always try to win the love of blond girls.

This man's subconscious mind earlier thought that this rejection meant he was unlikeable. This belief damaged his self-confidence, which his subconscious mind thought could only be restored by his being accepted by a blond girl.

In the same way, a man who dislikes his looks will surely fall in love with a beautiful girl, and a girl who unconsciously thinks that she is not safe will seek a strong man who can protect her, while a shy girl may fall in love with an assertive man.

In real life things aren't that simple, but the concept is the same. Some people fall in love just to compensate for their earlier failures and unmet needs. You may think that your partner is "the one," while in reality it's sometimes your past that makes you attracted to a certain person. If you could learn how to deal with those childhood experiences in an appropriate way, you would fall in love with people who are totally different from those you love now.

You may be crying over someone, thinking that he/she was your soul mate, while in reality it's your need to compensate for your weaknesses that's distressing you! A big part of love is based on compensating for our unmet needs and our past experiences. That's why a big part of the pain experienced after a breakup is related to the desire to compensate.

One good example that can illustrate this is how ostentatious men tend to fall in love with beautiful girls so they can complement their flashy appearance. When a pretentious person goes through a breakup he feels depressed until he finds another beautiful girl that makes him forget about his ex-partner.

Some people satisfy their compelling need to show off by having relationships with attractive girls. As soon as they lose them, they cry over them, thinking that it was true love. These people are usually compensating for the feelings of neglect which they suffered from in the past, or for the feelings of inferiority they are currently experiencing.

After a breakup, start to recall your partner's traits and see if he/she was a means of compensation for your weaknesses. If you realize this was in fact the case, you should know that once you learn how to deal with your personal issues, you won't need that partner anymore!

Even if you think that you need him/her, you should know that it's your subconscious mind tricking you into staying close to him/her, but you can outwit your subconscious mind by remembering that you felt you needed your partner due to your own personal flaws, not because of the love you feel towards that person.

The right thing to do – if this is actually your problem – is to be brave enough to admit your weaknesses and flaws and to start redressing them. If you don't do this and you leave these problems unresolved, one day they will result in another breakup.

Suppose that a very shy girl falls in love with a man because he is assertive and confident and thus fulfills her need to compensate for her weakness, what do you think will happen if one day she learns how to become assertive and confident in herself?

The end result is that she will no longer find herself attached to that person the way she was before simply because her need for compensation is diminished. That's why a lot of relationships that are based on compensating for weaknesses end in breakups. Compensation for your flaws is sometimes disguised as love.

Some older people even try to compensate for their lost youth by getting into relationships with young people. If you ask them about it, you may find they are not aware this is the reason for their attraction to people so many years younger than themselves. Other examples include people who try to compensate for the absence of a kind father or mother, or people who try to compensate for their insecurity.

Think about it: are you compensating for something? If even just a little bit of your answer is yes, then you should start dealing with this flaw right away and not let it be a reason for your life to depend on a relationship, either this one or the next.
Find ways to supplement what you are lacking.

If it's about boasting about what you have, start focusing on having more achievements; if it's about having a friend who cares about you, go out and meet more people to increase the chance of your meeting the right friend; and if it's about your insecurity, find ways to conquer it

Whatever it is and whatever you do, don't give in to your weaknesses because there are always ways to overcome them.

Self-Esteem Issues

Suppose that you went to your graduation party wearing a torn t-shirt and shorts and you noticed two people looking at you and whispering, wouldn't you think they were talking about you?

A human being's mind doesn't interpret the events that happen around us as they are, but instead it gives each event a meaning based on one's beliefs and ideas. In the previous example, you would think that they were talking about your t-shirt because you already knew that it was torn. On the other hand, if you were wearing a very expensive suit and the same people stared at you, you would probably have thought that they were envying your gorgeous clothes.

In other words, you don't see reality, but you rather see the reflection of your own thoughts and ideas. Now suppose that a person who thinks he/she is boring gets dumped. What do you think is the first thing that comes to his/her mind?

This person will think he/she was dumped because he/she is a dull person, and it's here precisely that the problem lies. The person already has an emotional wound and the breakup exposed it. That's why he/she is downcast after the breakup.

Do you see how significant this is?
In this case, it's a matter of self-pity rather than sadness over the loss of a partner. Therefore, the reason behind your desire to get back together with your ex-partner is to prove that you're perfect and thus eliminate the cause of self-pity.

If you can relate to this, I urge you to start reading and learning about how to solve your problem and to take steps towards setting it right. Any problem in the world can be analyzed and fixed. Take control of your life instead of allowing pain to take control of you.

This will not just help you with your break up; it will help you with many other areas of your life that self-pity sabotages.

When you find information that can help you, start practicing until you get the hang of dealing with your problems. According to NLP (neuro-linguistic programing), there are four stages of learning that we pass through before we master the thing we are trying to do. These are very interesting because they show you how you can actually do anything and that you will undoubtedly be able to do whatever it is well.

The first stage is called *Unconscious Incompetence*. At this very initial stage, a person knows nothing about a certain subject either consciously or unconsciously. That is, you don't know that such a thing exists.

The second stage is known as *Conscious Incompetence*. Here you recognize that this subject exists and that you are aware of it, but you know nothing about it.

A very common example here is learning to ride a bike. At the first stage you aren't even aware of the fact that you'll fall off if you try to ride your bike without help. At the second stage you realize that you need to learn how to ride it.

The third stage is called *Conscious Competence*. During this stage you learn what you need to know about a subject, but you still can't put it into practice. Although you have enough information, you can't easily apply it yet; you might have faced a similar situation when you were learning how to drive. Although you knew perfectly well what you should be doing, you still couldn't drive. You must have gotten confused and failed to drive well even though you knew the steps you were supposed to follow. This is because you were still driving on a conscious level.

Sadly, it is at this specific stage that many people give up, although if they were a little bit more patient, they would quickly move on to the next stage.

The final stage is called *Unconscious Competence*. After you've put in a lot of effort and practiced what you've learned, this skill will become your *"second nature,"* and now you'll be able to do it easily enough. Again, if we take the car example, you'll realize that at the final stage, you'll be able to drive without any mental effort because you do everything automatically.

Many people quit learning something before reaching the fourth stage, thinking that it's impossible to learn when it's actually just a matter of time.

Learn whatever you need to learn in order to remedy the real cause of your pain, give yourself plenty of time to learn it, and you'll be pleased when you realize that you have set many things in your life straight, not just the heartache caused by the breakup.

Back to the breakup, most people never know the real reason for being dumped, but since people see a reflection of their own thoughts in other people's behavior, they normally associate being dumped with the thing they like least about themselves.

Everyone does exactly the same thing when they're broken up with. The following are a few examples that illustrate how this happens:

- People who think they are not good-looking feel downcast after a breakup because they think they've been dumped because of their looks.
- People who think they are boring think that they have been dumped because of that.
- People who think they have problems expressing their feelings think this was the reason they've been dumped.

After a breakup people fixate on the things they hate most about themselves and blame the breakup on them. The conclusion is that some people become downcast after a breakup because it has exposed an emotional wound, not because they genuinely loved their ex-partners.

This means that if you're certain that you weren't dumped because of that specific reason, you won't be as upset as when you thought you were dumped because you have an unlikeable trait.

After a breakup, you should make sure that you aren't downcast because of this kind of emotional wound. If you realize that the wound is the main reason for your distress, you should know that it won't be difficult for you to get over your ex-partner.

I'm sure that by now you've started to realize that most of the things that make you feel depressed after a breakup are not related to the person who broke up with you, but rather to your own personal issues.

It is also worth mentioning what is known as "the act of retesting." Some people start to re-examine their personalities after a breakup in order to look for possible reasons that might have made their partners break up with them. It's as if the person is re-evaluating himself in order to find an explanation for what happened.

The problem with retesting is that it always leads the person to his emotional wounds and makes him/her associate them with the breakup. Sometimes having your self-confidence shattered hurts more than the breakup itself. Most people would be more at ease if they thought that they were dumped for a reason unrelated to their weaknesses.

External Dependency and Love

External Dependency is the term that refers to people who depend on external factors in order to regulate their moods or to forget their problems. Some people depend on cigarettes in order to feel in control. Others depend on drugs to escape bad moods, while others depend on love to be happy!

The problem with external dependency is that is does not solve any problems. It only removes them temporarily from your sight. When the external source of mood regulation is lost, the person usually finds life intolerable.

Yes, you may be in love with someone for a few years just because you're depending on the relationship to feel happy or to escape from your problems. You would then believe in such phrases as:

- Love is the solution to all my problems.
- I'm always down unless I'm in a relationship.
- I can't live without love.

Another problem with dependency on love is that it usually leads to falling in love with the wrong person. When mood regulation is the main incentive for choosing a partner, you disregard certain important factors that could destroy your relationship.

Suppose that you are severely depressed because you're going through a hard time in your life. Then you meet a cheerful girl who tries to help you get over all your problems. In this case, you may be attracted to and fall in love with her. But a few months later, when the problems are nowhere to be seen and you're feeling happy again, you will find that you don't need your partner and may decide to break up with her.

Surprisingly there are millions of relationships that are based on nothing but external dependency. In order to find out whether your relationship is built on external dependency or genuine love for your partner, ask yourself these questions:

Am I unhappy whenever I'm single?
Am I able to enjoy my life when I'm single?
Do I feel down unless I'm in a relationship?

If your answers are yes, you are certainly externally dependent on a relationship tin order o be happy. You should understand that emotional well-being is only achieved if you can feel good when you're single and feel better when you're in a relationship.

If you are externally dependent, the source of your pain after a breakup is not your having been dumped at all. You merely need someone else to make you feel happy. In that case, you should take serious actions towards dealing with your external dependency.

I know a girl who has always been dependent on a relationship to be happy. As long as I've known her, she has always been in one relationship or another. This did actually make her happy, but on the other hand, the problems which she'd been seeking refuge from in her relationships made her grow increasingly depressed, which in turn made her more dependent on a boyfriend to be happy.

At one point in her life, for a reason totally unrelated to her boyfriend, but rather because of work-related problems, she decided she wanted to snap out of her depression.

She started reading about how she could deal with her problems. For the first time in her life she persisted in fixing her problems – despite the fact that this seemed impossible to do – because she couldn't tolerate living unhappily anymore.

Having set her life straight, she has now spent four years without being in any relationship, which is something she's never dared to do in all the years I've known her. She doesn't have any urgent need to be with someone, and is prudently waiting for the right person.

Now she's calmer and enjoys great inner peace. She knows that for every problem there's a solution that can get rid of it if only she learns about it. She told me one day, "I decided I wouldn't allow myself to be downcast anymore. I've learned that anything can be dealt with if we only know how to deal with it."

I am not telling you this story to encourage you to stay without a partner for four years, but I am without a doubt telling you that fixing your life and dealing with your problems won't make you dependent on love as the only way to live happily.
Love is one of the most beautiful feelings you can experience, but love can be a curse rather than a blessing if your life suffers when you're not with someone.

Ask yourself these questions: "Why am I always so upset when I'm single? What is it that's making my life intolerable? What can I fix in order to be happy?"

Confronting yourself in this way needs a tremendous amount of courage, but it's the only way to get over external dependency. If you give in to external dependency, you will have to deal with the following consequences:

- You will only be accumulating problems without solving them.
- You will always fall in love with the wrong people.
- The next time you break up with someone you will feel ten times worse because of the accumulated problems that have been stacked up on your shoulders without being solved.

In short, dealing with a breakup may not require getting over your partner as much as dealing with the personal problems that were making you unable to tolerate being single. Overcome your problems so that you don't fall prey to external dependency. Only then can you enjoy healthy relationships.

Relationship Addiction

Do you like orange juice?
If you do, try drinking a glass of it each morning as soon as you wake up for twenty days. On the twenty-first day, don't drink any orange juice and see what happens.

You will most likely experience withdrawal symptoms because you have just lost something that you've gotten used to. The same thing will happen if you develop the habit of drinking coffee every morning and then suddenly quit.

So what does this have to do with love?
The hormones released by your body when you fall in love can cause a kind of addiction. When your body gets used to these hormones, you can experience withdrawal symptoms as soon as you fall out of love. The following are the things that people become addicted to in relationships:

- Phenylethylamine (PEA): A chemical that is responsible for the feelings of excitement you get when you are with your partner.
- Serotonins: Hormones that regulate the mood and make people feel happy.
- The emotional nurturing you used to receive from your partner.
- Saying and hearing phrases like, "I love you," or "I can't live without you."

When you say "I miss him/her," or "I can't forget about him/her," you could instead say without ruining the meaning, "I miss the PEA I used to get." or "I desperately need a dose of serotonin."

People think that they miss their ex-partners and that they can't live without them, while in reality they feel depressed when they are deprived of the chemicals they are addicted to. You might be saying, "That's nonsense – I was genuinely in love with my partner. A chemical has nothing to do with my feelings."

What determines whether or not your relationship was built on love addiction is not down to my opinion or yours, but the following signs. If you recognize them in yourself, you should know that you are a love addict, and that you don't miss your partner, but rather love itself.

- Not falling in love with a person unless he/she loves you first and then starting to develop feelings for him/her. This happens because you start to get addicted to the nice way he/she treats you.
- Falling in love often; people who fall in love very frequently are usually love addicts.
- Always feeling down when you're single.
- Always feeling downcast when you're alone.

As you may have already guessed, love addicts feel that life is intolerable without being in love or in a relationship; this usually causes them to make the wrong choices and to fall in love with the wrong people just to supply their bodies with the hormones and chemicals they need. They mistakenly think of their partners as their soul mates, while in reality it's their addiction to certain chemicals that made them fall in love with that person in the first place.

The great problem with love addiction is that it's always perceived as being real love, while it's only an addiction to something that you've grown used to. Love addiction can make a person unable to break up with his/her partner even if he hates lots of things about him/her.

The question you should ask yourself is, "Am I a love addict?"
And if your answer is "yes," it's time to dig for the reasons that have made you one. Are you missing love in your life? Are you often downcast and in need of someone to make you feel better?

You can't be a love addict unless you have an underlying problem influencing your behavior. The good news is that dealing with love addiction is not difficult; you just need to resist the urge to get into any relationship until the withdrawal symptoms are no longer there to fool you.

Love addiction is like any other type of addiction; you only need to quit the bad habit long enough for the chemicals to leave your body, and then you are no longer addicted. On the other hand, continuously jumping from one relationship to another will keep you addicted to love and prevent you from getting into a healthy relationship.

The Love Addiction Test

If you want a guideline in order to ascertain that you fully comprehend what is meant by love addiction, below is a simple test that can help you find out whether you are addicted to love. Think about each statement carefully and then tick either "Yes" or "No." When you have finished, calculate your score to find out the degree of your addiction or otherwise.

1. I pay a lot of attention to my romantic relationships so that I can cope with or escape from my problems.
   Yes__. No__

2. I believe that someone can fix me or make me better.
   Yes__ No__

3. I feel that I'm not truly alive unless I'm with my romantic partner.
   Yes__ No__

4. I don't have the energy to make my life better.
   Yes__ No__

5. I have often neglected my family/friends because of my relationship.
   Yes__ No__

6. I believe that being involved in a romantic relationship will make my life better.
   Yes__ No__

7. I am overwhelmed by loneliness when I'm not in a relationship.
   Yes__ No__

8. I feel that life is meaningless if I'm not in a relationship with someone I love.
   Yes__ No__

9. When one relationship ends I get into another one as soon as possible.
   Yes__ No__

10. I need to be in a romantic relationship to feel like a real man/woman.
    Yes__ No__

11. When I fall in love I'm unable to focus on the other areas of my life or carry on as usual. I can't help having romantic thoughts and fantasizing about my partner.
    Yes__ No__

12. I have always been preoccupied with love and romantic fantasies.
Yes__ No__

13. I sometimes think that there might be more I could do with my life if I weren't so caught up in my romantic pursuits.
Yes__ No__

14. I fall in love very easily.
Yes__ No__

15. I can't help becoming obsessed with my relationship when I fall in love.
Yes__ No__

16. I'm very lonely when I am single.
Yes__ No__

17. I have very few interests outside my relationship.
Yes__ No__

18. I believe that a romantic relationship is the solution to the problems in my life.
Yes__ No__

19. I sometimes lower my standards and settle for less than what I want for fear of being lonely.
Yes__ No__

20. First attraction is most appealing to me when choosing a partner. Falling in love over time is inevitable.
Yes__ No__

21. I frequently need reassurance from my partner in order to feel secure and confident.
Yes__ No__

22. When I get into a new relationship, I lose interest in activities that I normally enjoy.
Yes__ No__

23. I am usually depressed when I'm not spending time with my partner. I'm unhappy until I see him/her.
Yes__ No__

24. I tend to rush into love relationships without getting to know my partner.
Yes__ No__

25. I have difficulty liking myself and need constant reassurance from my partner in order to get a feeling of self-worth.
Yes___ No___

26. I tend to use a love relationship to make myself feel special.
Yes___ No___

27. I have difficulty setting appropriate boundaries in relationships. My partner has it his/her way most of the time.
Yes___ No___

28. I really fear not finding the right person for me and ending up alone.
Yes___ No___

29. I feel I don't want anyone to know about my romantic activities (i.e. the actions that I take to experience romance).
Yes___ No___

30. I believe that the problems in my love life are the result of my staying with the wrong person.
Yes___ No___

31. I wish I could control my romantic activities.
Yes___ No___

32. I have no self-control when I'm in love.
Yes___ No___

33. I'm quite needy in my relationship.
Yes___ No___

34. When I'm looking for a relationship I fall in love with almost anyone who shows the slightest interest in me.
a. Yes___ No___

35. I fall in love with the wrong people.
Yes___ No___

36. I fall in love with the wrong people to avoid being lonely.
Yes___ No___

37. When a relationship ends, I feel as if my life is over.
Yes___ No___

38. I can't say "no" to my partner.
Yes__ No__

39. If I am attracted to a person I ignore all the warning signs that tell me that he/she is not good for me.
Yes__ No__

40. I keep telling myself that my partner will get back to how he/she used to be at the beginning of our relationship despite all the evidence showing otherwise.
Yes__ No__

41. When I'm in love, I trust people who are untrustworthy, although I normally have difficulty trusting people.
Yes__ No__

42. I become so preoccupied with my partner's needs that I neglect my own.
Yes__ No__

43. I tend to give so much and take so little in return from my partner.
Yes__ No__

44. When I'm in love, I'm overly possessive and jealous.
Yes__ No__

45. I fear that my partner will find someone better than myself.
Yes__ NO__

46. I get into relationships with partners who are narcissists or have delusions of grandeur.
Yes__ No__

47. I go after the person I'm in love with even if he/she is involved with someone else. (Tick "yes" *only* if this is against your values in general, and you hate the fact that you sometimes do this.)
Yes__ NO__

48. Love and relationships are the only things that interest me.
Yes__ No__

49. I continue to cling onto a relationship even if it's unhealthy.
Yes__ No__

50. More than once I've found myself in a relationship that I was unable to end.
Yes__ No__

51. I'm excessively demanding in a relationship.
Yes__ No__

52. I can't say no to my partner if he/she threatens to leave me.
Yes__ No__

53. I would rather suffer emotionally than let go of a relationship.
Yes__ No__

54. I once got involved with someone who was unable to commit, hoping that he/she would change one day.
Yes__ No__

55. I get stuck in relationships that aren't going anywhere.
Yes__ No__

56. I once got involved with someone I couldn't leave.
Yes__ No__

57. I love romance. I've had more than one romantic interest at the same time.
Yes__ No__

58. I panic at the thought of being abandoned.
Yes__ No__

59. I chase after people who have rejected me and desperately try to change their minds about me.
Yes__ No__

60. When I'm in love, I lose the ability to make good choices.
Yes__ No__

61. I tend to compromise my beliefs and values to avoid being alone or abandoned.
Yes__ No__

62. I suffocate my partner because of my demanding attitude.
Yes__ No__

63. I tend to idealize my partner and see myself as being weaker and less important.
Yes__ No__

64. When a relationship ends, I get an urge to end my life.
Yes__ No__

65. I'm willing to bear neglect, depression, loneliness, dishonesty, and maybe even abuse to avoid the pain and anxiety of separation.

Yes__ No__

66. In some of my relationships I was the only one in love.
Yes__ No__

67. The slightest rejection makes me terrified of being abandoned.
Yes__ No__

68. Have you ever risked your reputation or financial stability for love?
Yes__ No__

Now it's time to calculate your score and analyze it.
Give yourself a zero for every "No" that you selected and add up the following scores for every "Yes":

Questions 1 – 5: give yourself **1** point for every "Yes" you answered.

Questions 6 – 26: give yourself **2** points for every "Yes" you answered.

Questions 27 – 45: give yourself **3** points for every "Yes" you answered.

Questions 46 – 63: give yourself **4** points for every "Yes" you answered.

Questions 64 – 68: give yourself **5** points for every "Yes" you answered.

Analyzing your answers:

If you've answered in the negative to all of the above behaviors, you should skip this section as you have proved to be free from love addiction. It's important to remember that it's normal to miss being in love and to look for your dream relationship. The problem occurs when this hampers your ability to lead a happy life.

What does it mean if I score 1s and 2s?
Scoring 1s and 2s doesn't mean that you're safe from becoming addicted to love. It indicates you can be addicted to certain aspects of a relationship. If you don't deal with your addictive tendencies, they will have a negative effect on your life, and certainly on your future relationships.

If you fall into this category of people, you should start dealing with your problems. These could be problems at work or at home, a need for intimacy or a need to feel special, for example. You've started depending on relationships to bring you joy and to bring a spark of hope to your life when you think there's nothing you can do to fix your problems.

However, you should be aware that if you don't deal with your problems, you'll be killing all your chances to lead a happy life and to enjoy the benefits of a healthy relationship.

If your need for intimacy is the reason for your addictive behavior, I advise you to develop more intimate relationships. This could be done by meeting new people, because the more people you meet, the greater your chance will be of finding people who share your interests and whose company you enjoy.

Therefore, you should fix your problems instead of relying on external factors to relieve your stress and satisfy your needs. Most problems appear insoluble because people don't take the time to work out how they can fix them. You should not let crises get a foothold in your life, but adapt to deal with the pain they cause you. Face them so that you'll be able to banish them from your life for good.

It's worth noting that you should never neglect the people and activities that you normally enjoy while you're in a relationship; this will make you more needy and dependent on your relationship for enjoyment. In other words, your relationship will be the source of all your happiness. This is why when you're in a relationship, you should continue to do the things and meet the people that you love in order to retain your individuality and independence.

If you depend on your relationship to feel special, you'll become heavily addicted to your partner and you may not be able to deal with being dumped. Therefore, the right thing to do is to make a list of all the things you need to change about yourself, and to start taking action to fix your life right now!

Lastly, you need to control the amount of time you spend fantasizing about your partner because this can make you exceedingly needy! So use your power to block out these thoughts for most of the day. This doesn't mean that you have to be cold-hearted or unromantic; it will only help you have a happy relationship without being needy.

What does it mean if I score 3s?
If you have scored 3s, the main reason for your addiction is *fear*. Let me establish a conditional rule here: If you don't calmly explain to your partner what upsets you and respect your own wishes and needs, he/she won't.

If you decide to grudgingly tolerate the things you dislike and never attempt to talk to your partner about them so that you can reach a compromise, you'll face exactly the things you are afraid of facing.

Being intolerant of whatever irritates or upsets you does not mean that you're being selfish. On the contrary, it means that you're aware that a healthy relationship is based on finding a middle ground with your partner. If your partner is the kind of person who refuses to consider your needs, your relationship will never be a healthy one. That's one unequivocal truth!

Don't resolve to tolerate mistreatment or inconsideration of your needs. If your partner is unwilling to make compromises for your sake, I'm sorry to tell you that it would be wise to leave him/her!

If you don't think highly of yourself, nobody will. You need to start with yourself; make a plan of all the things you want to change about your life and yourself, learn how you can do it and start right away.

If at the beginning of a relationship, you see a certain trait in your partner that's bound to turn the relationship into a nightmare later on, don't ignore your worries by insisting he/she is perfect regardless. If that trait persists, you should take it as a red light!

You can give the relationship a second chance, but if nothing changes, you should know it promises nothing but heartache and a lack of emotional well-being. It's then that you should come to the conclusion that it's not worth your while to stay with that partner.

One more piece of advice is not to get into a relationship with someone who doesn't like you the way you are, because you will exhaust your self-esteem trying to live up to his/her expectations. You can always find someone who likes you for who you are, especially if you decide to never stop improving the things you want to change about yourself.

If most of your scores are between 4s and 5s:
You are suffering from excessive love addiction.
Having answered the questions in the test, you now have a fairly good idea of your level of addiction. Nothing and no one in the world can change you or improve your life unless you determinedly decide to change.

Your case is an extreme one, but if you use the advice provided for the people who have scored less than you and in this book generally, you'll be surprised to see how quickly you start to thrive.

It's all a matter of decisiveness; I have seen so many people who were totally addicted to love change their lives. The problem lies in the fact that you love "*love*" itself. If you want to experience the love you unrealistically fantasize about, you must first intentionally come down to earth and make it happen.

Missing Love

If you generally miss love in your life, you will most likely become a love addict. Some people get into relationships not because they are in love with their partners, but because they crave the love that is absent from their lives.

Again, the subconscious mind plays the same trick; it makes it appear as if you've met a good catch, while the truth is that you are just trying to satisfy a certain need that you're deprived of, namely the need to be loved.

Some people think that their parents don't love them, others feel that their friends don't love them, while others think that no one loves them at all. I'm not saying that you are the one to be blamed if you are missing love in your life, because it's not your fault. Nevertheless, you should be able to separate this problem from your relationships so that it doesn't make you fall for the wrong person.

What is your relationship with your parents like?
How are your relationships with your close friends going?
Do you think that most people love you?
Do you think there is anybody who loves you?

By answering these questions, you'll be able to set this problem aside from your other emotions. Confusing your need to be loved with your other emotions will make you fall for someone you don't love just for the sake of restoring the missing love.

As you may have been able to work out by now, recovery from a breakup not only involves trying to stop thinking about your ex-partner or trying to be strong, but it also requires looking at the bigger picture and seeing that your relationship was your way of finding something that you're missing.

Missing love is very natural; all human beings have an urge to feel and give love. But if you can't live without being in a relationship, your addiction will make you very needy when you are in one. As we have established, there are many reasons that make someone desperately need a relationship. You need to find the reasons that are making your relationship with your ex-partner indispensable for you, and to start fixing them right away.

Fixing these things will not only make you experience a better and healthier relationship, but will also make you lead a happier life.

So it's alright to miss love, but it should also be alright to wait until you find the right person.

The Need for Approval

Some people who lack self-confidence and self-esteem need a constant source of external approval to help them feel good about themselves.

These people usually find life unbearable if that source of approval is taken away, and that's what makes their life miserable when they are single. They depend on their respective relationships just to feel the satisfaction of someone's approval even though they may not be genuinely in love with their partners.

All those months or years of crying over the partner who left you may be no more than your craving for the lost source of approval. If you find someone who provides you with the same amount of approval that your ex-partner used to give you, you'll forget about your ex-partner and fall in love with the new one!

Below are some common behavioral traits of people who get into relationships to satisfy their need for approval:

- They are extremely sensitive to criticism.
- They are excessively needy.
- They feel that something is going wrong if they don't hear the phrase, "I love you" at least a few times a day.
- They don't feel they are worthy unless someone loves them.
- They need constant reassurance that their partners love them.
- They need constant reassurance that they have good qualities.

There are millions of relationships that are built on seeking approval and acceptance from others. Sadly, in most cases, both partners are not aware of this fact; they mistakenly think they are each other's soul mates.

Knowing whether your feelings for a person are caused by your need for approval or by genuine love is a vital piece of information. Most of the relationships that are based on the need for approval end in a breakup because one partner usually finds a better source of approval and decides to split up with his/her partner.

If you have realized that one of the reasons you are in a relationship is to get your partner's approval, you should take serious steps towards building your self-confidence, motivated by the fact that this need for approval is making you fall in love with the wrong person.

When reasons other than genuine love cause you to get into a relationship, they distort your subconscious criteria in such a way that you might compromise some of your essential values and beliefs just to get into the relationship.

The need for approval, addiction to love and all of the other factors that we discussed earlier are very common in relationships. That's why many people always make wrong choices and go through a difficult time when trying to get over their partners. If it's your genuine, undying love for your ex-partner that's upsetting you, no advice will be able to relieve your pain or help you get over your partner, as you'll find yourself capable of accomplishing this goal all by yourself.

Before we get into the next section of the book, you need to think about whether you relate to any of the cases I mentioned earlier. Understanding the problem is half the cure; the rest is working on the issue itself, whatever that may be.

Once you start working on your problems, you won't only be ridding yourself of your breakup pain, but you'll also be giving your mind clues to be able to choose a good match for you in the future.

The root causes of your problems affect many aspects of your life; if there's one problem you're not dealing with, it will probably affect your work, your family, your friends, and your other relationships. Fixing one of your problems will automatically improve the rest of your life.

As I have mentioned before, problems seem nearly impossible to fix at the beginning, but if you read and learn more about how to solve them, you will come to see that you have been overestimating their seriousness. Therefore, avoiding inertia and taking the initiative is the key to improving all the aspects of your life.

When you take the first step, your brain will readily help you overcome or learn whatever you need. You'll be surprised to see how much you can achieve if only you make the first move. It's all about starting.
Many people fail to recognize their potential just because they have never attempted to take the first step. Don't be one of them.

Start reading and collecting information about your problem. There are now answers to almost any questions you might have. Look for them, or ask experienced people and start dealing with your problem right now.

Now that you have identified what you need, you can move on to the next step.

The Stages of Recovery

After a breakup, everyone passes through certain phases of recovery:

- Denial
- Anger
- Bargaining/Depression
- Acceptance
- Recovery

The only difference between those who recover after a few days and those who take years to recover is how fast they pass through each phase. Let's examine each phase and see how you can recover from it quickly.

Denial: Denial is the first stage; this is the stage when you refuse to accept that the breakup has actually taken place. In other words, you are reluctant to admit that the breakup is real. You will probably say something like, "Maybe he/she didn't mean it. I'll call him/her again to make sure," or "Maybe he/she said that because he/she was angry. He/she could never dump me like that."

Denial usually lasts for a short period of time unless you intentionally try to fool yourself. As soon as you doubt something, you should attempt to prove it, and that's when you move on from denial to the next stage, which is anger.

Anger: "I'll make him pay for it. I'll make sure he/she regrets dumping me. How could he/she leave me?" The anger phase doesn't last long either. Actually, both denial and anger can last just a few hours before you move on to the third and most dangerous stage, namely bargaining.

Bargaining: The bargaining stage is what determines who recovers from a breakup in a few days and who might take years to recover. All of the other stages have a limited time span – even after the worst breakup – but the bargaining stage has no defined limit, and so some people can remain stuck in it for years.

Bargaining is the stage when someone has very little hope, somewhere between 5 and 95% loss of hope. Believe it or not, it's the 5% that makes you feel downcast, not the 95%, because the more certain you are that your relationship cannot work, the easier it will be for you to move on to the next stage. Both bargaining and depression are part of the same phase, when your mood keeps shifting from the hope of getting your partner back to depression, and vice versa.

The bargaining stage is characterized by the following behavior:

- Going to the same places you used to go to with your ex-partner hoping to see him/her by coincidence.

- Listening to music that keeps feeding your mind ideas such as, "I can't live without my love," or "my life is meaningless without my other half."
- Rushing to your phone whenever it rings hoping that your ex-partner is the one calling you.
- Day dreaming of living happily ever after with your ex-partner.
- Begging your ex-partner to take you back. Asking him/her to give your relationship a second chance to see if you can get along.

As long as you keep bargaining you can never recover. Your subconscious mind keeps vacillating between hope and despair, until you finally realize that the relationship is truly over.

So what should you do exactly in order to get over the bargaining stage? The simple actions that you should take are the following:

- Ask your partner straight if there's any hope of your getting back together or make a friend ask him/her. That way, you'll have closure.

- If the relationship ended with an email or a text message, you should call your partner and repeat the break up over the phone, even if he/she is living in another country. You should know that as long as there is even 1% uncertainty in you, you'll never recover. Try to make the breakup tangible so you can put all your doubts to rest

- Stop listening to music and watching movies that might brainwash you and make you think you can't live without your partner.

- Stop hoping to fix your relationship with your partner and stop day dreaming.

- Don't go to the same places you used to go to with your partner unless you really have to. If you do go, try not to think about him/her while you are there.

- Stop thinking about him/her. You might think that you can't help it, but you should remember that you have control over what thoughts occupy your mind for more than a few seconds. You can effectively banish any thought from your mind just a few seconds after it pops up.

- Throw away any pictures of your ex-partner, as well as any gifts from him/her. Delete his/her text messages to remove all traces of the relationship. Although if you still have any boxes of chocolate that your partner gave you, you should eat them instead of throwing them away.

Doing this might upset you at first, but within a few days you'll discover that not taking these actions would have stood in the way of your recovery. Suppose your ex-partner, who you once couldn't get over at all easily, decides to get married and invites you to his/her wedding, what should your response be?

Contrary to common belief, going to the wedding is the right thing to do because it sends a signal to the subconscious mind that your relationship is irrevocably over, and that you should move on from the bargaining stage to that of acceptance.

A friend of mine once had a long-distance relationship. When her partner broke up with her in an email, she didn't call him for weeks because she didn't want to face the truth. The mistake my friend made was that she lingered in the bargaining stage for six months just because she didn't want to accept that the relationship had ended.

If she had carefully assessed the situation, she would have discovered that the pain she had to endure for those six months was a hundred times worse than the feelings she would have experienced if she had attempted to have closure. The pain she would have felt after her breakup wouldn't have lasted for more than a few days before going away.

The bargaining stage is the most important stage in the recovery process. If you manage to get over it in a few days, you should know that your problem is solved.

If you are determined to get over your ex-partner, decide now to stop hoping that you might get back together. Stop tormenting yourself with lots of "What ifs," and even worse, "That could happen."

Like I said, if you stop that train of thought, you should know you are on the right track, and that you'll be over your ex-partner very soon.

This is *the* most critical part. If you deal with it wisely, you can assure yourself that the worst is over.

Acceptance: When you take in the fact that that there's no hope of getting back together with your ex-partner, you'll feel distressed, but then you'll start to accept the breakup. Acceptance can only take place when you feel certain that there are no other options but acceptance. If you think that there's the tiniest chance of your getting back together, you can never reach the acceptance phase. Loss of hope is the message that your subconscious mind needs in order to start accepting any unpleasant fact.

But the most important question you should have asked yourself is, "Doesn't loss of hope lead to depression?" The difference between loss of hope and depression is that you can only become depressed if you know that you've lost someone who you can never replace.

If you have an empty bank account and you lose the last 10 dollars you had to buy food, you'll become depressed because you know you have no other source of income. On the other hand, if you have a million dollars in your bank account and you lose a thousand dollars, you'll be upset only for a few minutes or hours before you completely forget about this setback.

Depression affects us because of the false ideas that the media feeds us regarding the concept of "the one" or "the soul mate." How could you not become depressed after a breakup if you've been led to believe that there's only one good match for you in the whole world? In other words, depression is inevitable when you think that you've lost an irreplaceable love.

Recovery: When you recover from a breakup you will find yourself stronger than before. The relief you experience after recovery makes you forget about the turmoil that you've been through, and you'll only remember the knowledge that you've gained from your experience. Recovery is characterized by feeling better day by day, until you suddenly realize that you can describe yourself as happy and contented again.

Do I finally let go? Is that it?

If you have tried and finally understood that there can be no reversal of the breakup, you should stop bargaining. Many people keep going back to their ex-partners and breaking up many times even though they know they're fooling themselves.

I understand how difficult it is to break up with your loved one, but please bear with me and answer the following questions:

- Did you try many times to make the relationship succeed?
- Are there any issues that one or both of you are unwilling to deal with or fix?
- Do you know there are certain problems that will never be resolved but you still choose to act as if they aren't there?
- Do you feel dissatisfied because you're not getting most of the things you need from your partner but you're still hanging on to him/her?

Of course you should always try very hard to mend your relationship with your partner, and many people succeed in doing so. But if you have answered in the affirmative to some or all of the above questions, I think that giving your relationship any more chances would be of no avail.

If you refuse to let go of a dead-end relationship, you should know you are in the denial stage, when you still can't believe that your relationship is over. Ask yourself if this is how you want your love life to be indefinitely.

If you answer in the affirmative, you don't really want to get over your partner. But if it it's not what you want, you shouldn't bargain or keep yourself hanging between hope and acceptance.

This question usually comes to mind during the first stages of a breakup, when you can't believe that your relationship is over. But it's an absolutely crucial question. A whole chapter is devoted to it because it can cause someone to bargain for a very long time and get stuck in this stage.

Is it really over? Do I finally let go?
If you answered "yes" to the above questions, let me reassure you, "Yes, it is really over and you need to let go of your relationship."

It's not the end of the world; breaking up with your partner is not the worst thing that can happen to you.

When you get used to something, your brain dislikes and often resists any change because it doesn't like the uncertainty that accompanies it. Your brain is repelled by the fact that it will now have to modify its methods of managing your life and learn how to deal with your changed lifestyle all over again. Knowing this, I understand the turmoil you're going through.

If, however, you're aware of the workings of your mind, you might be able to make your brain relent and come to terms with the undesirable change. Change may also begin to appear less horrifying if you plan for your future.

Sometimes we don't change from fear of change itself. Have you ever heard of the snowball effect?
Let me give you an example:

Oh my God, it's four p.m.!
I have to be there in 10 minutes at the most.
But what if I don't arrive on time!
I might miss part of the exam. That's terrible; I can't afford to lose any more marks.
And if I don't do well in this exam, it'll be fatal for me!
And if get a bad grade in one more subject, I could fail this entire year!
And if I don't graduate now I might not be able find a job later on! There seems to be a recession coming on.

Right there you should say, "Stop!"
You see in this example a person who is only 10 minutes late for an exam, but is already thinking about failing and the approaching recession!

The irony lies in the fact that, although this train of thought seems amusing to read here, we often unconsciously think in a similar way. It starts with a small seed, which the unwanted event produces. Negative thinking then turns the small seed into a big tree and sometimes a forest!

These negative thoughts create fears and make the problem seem more monstrous than it truly is, which in turn makes you feel impotent, resenting change and remaining idle. Don't fail prey to your fears because they are like a magnifying lens which makes you see your problems bigger than they actually are.

Instead of standing helplessly by, staring at change in horror, I advise you to think. Plan the new situation well to save yourself the anxiety of facing something that you are unprepared for. This step will also help you manage your life better.

You are neither the first nor the last person to go through a breakup. Be one of the millions that have gone through one but were also able to turn over a new leaf.

Learn from the Ants

Ants are insects that work very hard to reach their goals. They are tiny, but what they succeed in doing is absolutely astounding. The secret to succeeding in achieving your goal is to start now and to take only one step at a time.

The ant is nature's average Joe, as they say, but even an average Joe can turn into a superhero.

If you decide to face your breakup with a good plan and to work your way through it step by step, you'll be able to recover in a short space of time. If you leave food out where ants can reach it, they will only take tiny pieces of it at first, but after some time they'll have taken a big portion.

Do you know that these little creatures have been estimated by scientists to have been living on earth for more than 100 million years? Their capacity for organization and production has astonished scientists over the years. Impressed by their abilities, we human beings tend to imitate their behavior in order to thrive as they do.

One thing that ants force us to realize is that even if a situation demands more than your physical or emotional attributes permit you to, you can deal with it if you make a one-step-at-a-time plan. Don't overwhelm yourself with unrealistic resolutions. Be like the ants, who know that despite their weakness they can achieve anything.

Every small act of persistence counts. It's the consistency of your efforts – insignificant as they may seem – that can achieve the impossible.

Don't say, "What's the worst that can happen if I just quickly check his/her webpage once?" or "What harm can it be if I give him/her just one call?"

Every small action counts, so make it count in your favor, not against you.

Close the Doors and Lock Them

As I have said before, it's the lingering hope that they might make it up with their partner that prevents people from recovering fast from breakups. Some people end relationships, but leave the door ajar, hoping that they might get back together with their partner one day.

Leaving the door ajar leaves one hope alive, which in turn infects you with the inability to recover from the breakup. The correct thing to do, therefore, if you are determined to recover, is to close all the doors that might lead you back to your partner by confirming with him/her that your breakup is irrevocable.

The way you close the doors depends on your current relationship with your ex-partner; if you're on good terms, you can call him/her to hear that this was the right decision to make and in this way relinquish your hope.

If your relationship with your ex-partner ended with a fight – which is something that happens quite often – you should text him/her to say that you don't regret the breakup.

I'm not asking you to use a certain template to close the doors, because every case is different from the others. However, a generalization can be made by saying that leaving doors ajar will delay or even prevent recovery from *any* breakup.

By "close the doors and lock them," I mean reassure yourself and your partner that the breakup can never be retracted. If you've taken the decision to get over your ex-partner, tell yourself never to look back; what is done cannot be undone. Therefore, you should block any thoughts of being reunited with your ex-partner once they put in an appearance in your mind.

Getting over someone is not a hard thing to do at all *if* you've taken the decision to do it. Bargaining and indecision are what make it seem painful. You should not, therefore, give in to these states of mind. Reflect on the matter, and if you conclude that this relationship is not right for you, close the doors and lock them to kill your doubts and stop your dithering.

The question that people usually ask here is, "How can I weigh things up properly so I know for sure if the relationship is not right for me?"
That's a good question.
Well, let me ask you this, "With the exception of the good memories, are you happy and satisfied with your relationship? Is your partner doing anything to fix it?"

If your answer is "yes," you should hold on to your relationship and try to repair it. Only stop trying when it becomes utterly pointless to try.

But if you're unsatisfied and your partner is unresponsive to your attempts to mend your relationship, you should know it's not a healthy one. Maybe it's time you had second thoughts about it.

Of course, if you have already broken up with your partner, don't keep doubting your decision. Close all the doors and burn all the bridges that can lead you back to your partner, and don't try to look back.
It's as simple as that.

Rebound Relationships

After any loss, nothing looks better than a chance for victory, and that's why a lot of people make hasty decisions which they regret later.

Right after breakups, people start to feel that they've lost a good source of intimacy, someone who cared for them and made their lives happy. Desperately trying to restore this situation, some people get into a new relationship right after breaking up. This is what is otherwise known as a rebound relationship.

The person seeking a rebound relationship usually does so to compensate for the absence of his/her ex-partner. Rebound relationships can also begin just before a breakup, when it's clear that the original relationship will inevitably end soon. In this case, the main purpose of the rebound relationship is to prevent you from experiencing the pain you feel after a breakup.

Some people seek rebound relationships because they are addicted to love. Fearing loneliness, they look for people who can make them feel lovable and special. While these might sound like valid reasons, they are clear signs of relationship addiction. When falling in love has the sole purpose of not feeling lonely, it's never based on real love; it's only a way of lifting your mood and helping you cope.

One of the main causes of rebound relationships is love addiction. When a love addict loses his/her source of positive emotions, the withdrawal symptoms will make him/her want to start a rebound relationship. The subconscious mind, in this case, seeks the happiness that comes with a new relationship, and the result is a short-lived rebound relationship.

Sometimes people seek rebound relationships to prove to themselves that they are lovable, especially when they are not the ones responsible for the breakup. Finding someone in love with them as soon as their relationship ends serves as irrefutable proof of the worthiness of their love and affection.

Seeking a rebound relationship can happen on both the conscious or unconscious level. When it happens consciously, you are aware of your goal, namely restoring your self-worth. On the other hand, if it happens unconsciously, you will suddenly find yourself in a new rebound relationship, thinking that your new partner is "the one."

If you don't know how to deal with a breakup because you are always driven by your emotions, you will have the tendency to form rebound relationships. In this case, the main aim of the rebound relationship will be to spare you the pain that the breakup has caused.

After a breakup, people, especially women, usually experience intense emotional instability. This instability can result in bad decisions, leading them to rush into short-term rebound relationships. A generalization claiming that *all* rebound relationships have no prospects would be mistaken, but we can say for sure that a relationship that is based on emotional stability is a lot healthier than a rebound relationship.

My advice for you is if you've just broken up with your partner or got divorced, is to give yourself a rehabilitation period. Resist any temptation to seek comfort in a new relationship. If you get into a rebound relationship, you'll start comparing your ex-partner with your new one. Your ex-partner will most likely win, and so you'll feel inclined to end the new relationship when it dawns on you that you are not genuinely in love with your new partner.

If you learn how to overcome love addiction, you'll only start a new relationship when you have genuine loving feelings for a person, not when you want to feel lovable. Rebound relationships are almost always short term and rarely succeed. Give yourself some time to recover from a relationship before starting a new one, because the only action that can never cause any damage is patience.

Nobody is Ever Like Him/Her

Some people who start new relationships directly after breakups find themselves constantly comparing their new partner with their ex-partner. All the problems occur when the comparison ends in favor of the ex-partner. This reinforces in your mind the idea that your ex-partner is the irreplaceable "soul mate."

The reasons that could make your ex-partner win a comparison are:

- Your love for your new partner is not genuine.
- Your ex-partner was a better match to meet your subconscious criteria. (Remember this does not mean there aren't any better matches for you.)
- You are addicted to relationships and you've rushed into a new one after your breakup only because you can't tolerate being alone, not because you are in love.
- The new relationship is only a rebound relationship born from your emotional instability and is therefore lacking in validity.

To sum up, you might think that your ex-partner is a better match for you, not because he/she is perfect and irreplaceable, but because your current partner is not a good match for you. In other words, if your ex-partner seems a better match for you, you should know your choice of partner in your current relationship was hasty and therefore mistaken.

Your ex-partner is not the best one in the world, and there are lots of people who are much better than him/her. If your current partner is not one of them, this is because you have made a wrong choice. When other people don't compare with your ex-partner, it doesn't mean that your ex-partner's goodness is unsurpassable; it only means that you haven't yet met someone who can supersede him/her.

But We Were So Similar to Each Other!

Let me remind you of the example where a man goes out wearing a torn t-shirt and notices two people whispering to each other and looking at him. He thinks they are talking about his torn t-shirt, doesn't he?

Now, suppose that he's wearing his best outfit and the same thing happens. He now thinks that those people are talking about how fashionable his clothes are, correct?

Our minds follow a rule called, "You get what you focus on." The people may not have been talking about his torn t-shirt or his nice clothes; they may have even been talking about something unrelated to him. However, our minds try to find clues that prove the things we are thinking about, and so we never actually see the truth, but only a reflection of our own beliefs and ideas.

Your mind receives billions of pieces of information per second, but it discards most of them and only keeps 7-9 pieces which it thinks are relevant. For example, you are now reading this book and focusing on the words in it, but I'm sure that you are also aware of the color of your computer, the noises in the background, the lighting in the room, the voices of any people talking nearby, and the feel of your back against the chair or sofa. From all of this information, your conscious mind only keeps what is relevant while the rest is discarded.

Do you remember the example of a man who buys a new car and suddenly starts seeing that same brand everywhere? When you buy a new car or a new mobile phone you think that everybody you come across has bought it too because your new possession has been classified by your mind as relevant information to be focused on, not discarded. You've always seen people driving the same car or using the same phone, but this has been irrelevant to you until you owned one yourself.

What does this have to do with this chapter? When you fall in love with someone your mind starts to look for all the similarities between you in order to convince you that this person is a good match. Therefore, the discarding mechanism avoids drawing your attention to many of the dissimilarities, and only focuses on the many things you have in common.

The result of this mental activity is usually good if the relationship is destined to continue. However, a problem occurs when a breakup takes place because the two partners start thinking, "But we're so similar to each other. How can I find another person like him/her?"

Reem Ismail, the co-author of this book, declared that she'd made the same observation about her past relationships. In each relationship, she thought that her partner was her counterpart. That's what hurt her most after each breakup.

After breaking up with each of her partners, she used to get upset, thinking it would be impossible to find anyone as similar to her as her ex-partner. Each partner was similar to her regarding a certain aspect; sometimes it was because he shared her dreams, sometimes it was because he'd had the same experience of having to move to different countries while growing up, and sometimes it was because he lived in the same neighborhood as her and his parents were similar to hers.

Her false belief of the impossibility of her meeting another counterpart was destroyed when she met several other partners who were similar to her in different ways. She now believes that you can easily find a lot of counterparts, but what is more important is finding a counterpart who meets your subconscious, indispensable criteria. She's convinced that it's naïve to think that you can never find your counterpart because you can always meet new people who share your traits, beliefs or lifestyle.

As you must have worked out by now, the perceived similarity between yourself and your ex-partner is nothing other than the result of a filtering process that your mind has gone through. I'm not implying that you have nothing in common; if there were no similarities between you, you wouldn't have fallen in love with each other in the first place. What I mean to say is that your biased perception of your similarity to your ex-partner is clouded by your love for him/her and the resulting actions of your subconscious mind.

In short, if you think that you were 99% identical to your ex-partner, the truth is that you were only 20% identical. There are millions of other people out there who could be more similar to you than him/her because a 20% identical match is very easy to find.

As soon as you break up with someone, start to think of your differences. If you can pinpoint these, you'll reach the conclusion that you were fooled by your subconscious mind. Also, remember that it's not the end of the world to lose a counterpart, as you are bound to meet many others.

It's all in your mind; change your false belief about the impossibility of finding your dream partner, because this alone could hold you back from finding him/her. There are hundreds and thousands of people that you haven't met yet, and so many of them you'll find to be just as likeable and similar to you.

Losing What You Possess

Sometimes the main reason some people are upset after a breakup is the loss of what they used to possess. We all have the desire to possess things, but when this desire infiltrates our relationships, it turns them into unhealthy ones, sustained merely by our desire to be in control of the things we possess.

People who have a strong desire to possess things usually do their best to get back their relationship with their partner after a breakup, not because of their genuine love for their partner, but because they feel that they have lost one of their possessions.

I have personally met many people who don't necessarily want their partner back because they genuinely love them, but because they think that their partner belongs to them, and they can't stand watching someone else take something that is theirs. They keep checking their social network pages and following their news because they feel that they own him/her. Of course it's impossible to get over someone if you're thinking, "But he's mine! He's mine! How can he be with someone else?"

Being in love with a person who loves you back doesn't mean that he/she is yours, so you should put this thought out of your head. Yes, he/she may have belonged with you at some time in the past, and yes, your relationship may have been very intimate, but this doesn't mean that you have ownership of this person.

Ridiculous as it may sound, being hurt due to breaking up with your partner can be compared to being upset when you lose your wallet or your mobile phone. However, you don't keep crying over your phone for years, because you know that the loss is irreversible. The problem with relationships is that there is always the chance of bargaining and the possibility of undoing the breakup. That's why people keep suffering instead of recovering.

A girl once told me that she had managed to deal with her breakup well until she found out that her ex-partner was in a relationship with someone else. It was then that she was seized by an uncontrollable desire to get back together with him and couldn't get over her anguish. Her actual words were, "I didn't want him back when we broke up and I was doing absolutely fine. I don't know what came over me when he started dating her."

When we spoke about it and put the matter into perspective, she realized that her possessiveness was the driving force making her long for her partner, and so it became easier for her to make the decision to let go of the relationship and to start blocking all thoughts about her partner. This was after I had asked her, "Honestly, is this the person you *really* want?"

Understanding your situation more clearly always makes you think straight and able to make wise decisions. Always reflect on what you can relate to from the cases I've mentioned in this book, and then make the decision to remedy your situation. It's only a matter of making that decision.

You might, unlike the girl I mentioned above, have wanted to be reunited with your partner right after you broke up, but that doesn't mean your feelings didn't arise from your sense of ownership. Ask yourself, "Am I holding onto my partner because I feel he/she belongs to me, and not because I sincerely want to be with him/her?"

After a breakup you should stay away from your ex-partner for at least one week. If your attachment is rooted in your desire to possess him/her, time will dissolve it.

Confusing Guilt with Love

Your mind is always engaged with the process of encountering new situations, which allows you to forget about the unfinished business of the past. For example, if you were disliked by your schoolmates when you were a child, you might become an extremely sociable adult.

Whenever you a meet a new person, your subconscious mind convinces you that you must succeed in doing what you failed to do in the past. That's why it's made you eager to meet new people in the first place; your subconscious mind wants you to forget about your past by compensating for it in the present.

The problem with this defense mechanism is that you are usually not aware that you're doing a certain action because of your unresolved childhood complexes, and that's why you might mistake your feelings for what they are not.

One of the strongest unresolved complexes is guilt. If you were rude to your little sister when she was in need of your help, your subconscious mind will make you fall in love with a girl who looks like your sister to allow you prove to yourself that you can be a kind person.

In this case, the main driving force behind love is nothing other than *guilt!* However, you won't realize that it's your guilt making you fall in love with that particular person. Instead you'll think that every girl you are attracted to is "the one" who you can't live without, not a girl who is boosting your own ego.

Confusing love with guilt is very common in relationships; there are a lot of relationships based on the guilt factor. Of course, guilt isn't the only reason relationships start, but it's one of the strongest pillars holding them up.

In addition to accumulated guilt, you might become attached to someone who succeeds in making you feel guilty. For example:

- If your partner has shown you that he/she is in real need of being with you forever.
- If your partner has been through a hard time.
- If your partner makes you think that he/she will be depressed forever if you leave him/her.
- If your partner has done you an emotional or a material favor.

Any of these factors is enough to trigger the guilt factor, and can make you reluctant to break up with your partner. The smartest of us confuse guilt with love, so if you want to know whether your feelings can be defined as love or as guilt, you should ask yourself the following question:

"Was guilt one of the reasons I was upset after the breakup? Was guilt one of the incentives for getting back together with my partner?"

If you answered in the affirmative, you should realize that your relationship was not built on love, but guilt.

Remember that emotions are transient; "the one" is non-existent. Hang on to this fact when your guilt becomes overwhelming. Be aware that if you are with someone for the sole reason that you think you're doing him/her good, you will, one day, be doing him/her harm.

There will come a day when you won't be satisfied and your unmet needs will lead you to look for more than what you have now. When this happens, inevitable as it is, you'll be harming your partner instead of helping him/her.

If the only pillar holding up your relationship is your providing moral support for your partner, you should bear in mind that the two of you will end up being hurt. Will leaving him/her hurt more? Yes, but it will hurt a lot more if you cling on to the relationship despite not being genuinely in love with your partner.

Think of the least hurtful way to terminate the relationship. Never ignore a problem just because you think it's insoluble. You should always choose the least of two evils. A relationship needs two fully committed people; if one of the two partners doesn't want the relationship anymore, it's best for *both* of you to end it.

When you talk to your partner, don't get into blame-finding because there's always wrong on both sides. When breaking up, you should sit down face-to-face with your partner and avoid breaking up over the phone or in an email unless there are certain reasons to do it that way, such as living in different countries or that it's better for your partner. Your guilt shouldn't come from ending the relationship, but by deluding your partner into thinking he/she is loved. Not confronting your partner with the truth means betraying his/her trust in you. A calm talk with your partner about the impossibility of your staying together will resolve any difficulty arising from the situation.

If your partner has some questions, answer them as honestly as you can without delivering any emotional blows. Breaking up is not about finding whose fault it is; it's about your being able to find closure to this relationship so that you are both able to move on.
So try to comfort your partner and be kind to him/her, but be firm about ending the relationship.

Confusing Stubbornness with Love

In my book, "How to Make Someone Fall in Love with You," I described a technique that can make a stubborn person become attached to you. It's called "Triggering Stubbornness." By telling a stubborn partner that people think your relationship together won't last, you'll trigger the stubborn part of their personality and so fuel their best attempts to prove those people wrong.

Sometimes people confuse stubbornness with love. In other words, their stubbornness prevents them from seeing that they are not head over heels in love with their partners. After a breakup, you should examine your feelings to see if one of the things keeping you attached to your partner is stubbornness. These clues can help you better determine whether stubbornness is one of the things preventing you from getting over your partner:

- Are you overly concerned about what people will say after they hear about your breakup?
- Are you embarrassed to face the people who predicted that this relationship wouldn't last?
- Do you want to prove to everyone that you weren't dumped?
- Do you want to prove to others that the relationship could continue despite the differences between you and your partner?
- If you were living on a desert island alone with your partner, would it still hurt you to break up with him/her?

Your subconscious mind is very intelligent; it won't allow you to think that only your stubbornness is keeping you with your partner, instead it will convince you that you are genuinely in love with him/her. Asking yourself the above questions can help you find out about the small tricks that your resourceful subconscious mind is playing on you. There are millions of reasons why some people fail to get over their ex-partners. Stubbornness is one of them.

Are You Codependent?

Out of a desire to feel needed and a lack of self-esteem, some people try to hold onto their relationships, even when they are a source of pain to them. Staying in an emotionally abusive or unhealthy relationship is not unusual for a codependent person.

Codependent people find it excessively difficult to get over breakups because their relationships satisfy some of their basic needs, namely feeling worthy, needed and self-confident.

The loss of a relationship to a codependent person means the loss of their self-confidence. That's why they feel great pain just thinking about breaking up. The following signs can help you know if you are a codependent person:

- Feeling responsible for other people's problems.
- Feeling guilty when you can't help a person in need.
- Having low self-esteem.
- Trying to control people.
- Being very sensitive to criticism.
- Suppressing your emotions instead of confronting your partner with them.
- A tendency to look for those who need help.
- An intense fear of rejection.
- An intense fear of abandonment.
- Feeling insecure.
- Having a feeling of inadequacy.

Dealing with codependency is a must if you want to get over someone. The question you should ask yourself is, "Do I love that person or do I just need him/her?" If you realize that you only need your partner in order to help you deal with your personal flaws, you'll be able to work out that it's not your partner who can make you feel happy, but the courage to face your problems and the strength to deal with them.

You should start to focus on developing self-confidence so that you become less dependent on other people's approval. Once you do so, you won't become attached to a relationship that is harmful for your emotional well-being. The key to dealing with codependency is developing self-confidence.

Resist the Urge

One of the things that stop people from mending their broken hearts is that they fail to resist the urge to stop bargaining. Either through phone calls, emails, text messages or even fantasizing, they keep trying to restore their relationship, even if they're certain that they are doomed to fail.

The problem with this kind of behavior is that it will always leave the subconscious mind expecting the relationship to be fixed, which in turn will subject you to great disappointment. Some people force themselves to become strong enough to end their relationships, but after a few hours they find themselves unable to tolerate the pain, and so they start to bargain again.

One important thing you should know is that this pain will only last for a few days before it completely disappears. The only reason why it failed to disappear sooner is that you had taken the decision to keep bargaining.

Coming to terms with the fact that breaking up with your partner will cost you some pain will help you tolerate it for a few days, after which it will dissipate. If you decide to bargain, on the other hand, your pain will last indefinitely.

That's why people think that the pain after a breakup will never end; they feel depressed for a few days then prolong their agony by deciding to bargain. In short, if you want to recover from your breakup in a few days, you should have closure in order to prevent you from thinking about the possibility of going back to your partner.

Resist the urge to get in touch with him/her or to find out his/her news. In other words, if you've taken the decision to get over someone, you should have self-discipline.

Most human beings like to experience the feeling of love and being with someone. However, like everything else, if relationships are not dealt with properly, they can harm us. It's not what you do, but how you do it. Love is a double-edged sword; it can make us happy if we know how to manage it, but it can also hurt us when we mess with it.

If your relationship is not meant to be, you should stop bargaining and control your desire to experience the euphoria of love. Be patient, because you will eventually meet the right person who will make you feel the joys of falling in love.

Controlling Your Thoughts

Thoughts are fundamentally arbitrary and uncontrollable. Despite your attempts to ban your mind from thinking about someone, you might see something that reminds you of a certain person and end up thinking about him/her all day long.

Very small things – such as a phrase, an object or a person – can remind you of your ex-partner, provided that they are associated in your mind with him/her.

If the thinking process is beyond our control, yet we have to control it in order to quit thinking about someone, how can we get over our ex-partners?
The answer is simple: Although the thinking process may seem out of control at first, you can gain full control over it in just a few minutes.

For example, if you see an advertisement for your favorite chocolate on your way back home while you are on a diet, you can either stop thinking about the advertisement, or you can start picturing yourself eating the chocolate and giving up on your diet for one day.

In a similar way, many things can remind you of your ex-partner. You can either shut them away or give in to them. People give in by day dreaming, by picturing themselves with their ex-partner, and by looking for yet more things that remind them of their ex-partner. If you give in to these thoughts, you will enter an endless cycle of recalling certain memories and getting upset.

Think of your feelings for your ex-partner as a seed that is watered whenever you remind yourself of it. If you want to forget about him/her, you should avoid watering the seed. In this way you guarantee its death within a few days. People usually fail to stunt the growth of these seeds because they water them every now and then by reminiscing about their ex-partner.

Their minds become full of thoughts about the wonderful feelings they used to experience with their partner, and picture how things might have been if they hadn't broken up. When these thoughts take control of their minds, they easily give in to the impulse to day dream and reminisce constantly.

Many people are aware that the reason for giving in is due to their being weak and unable to get over their ex-partner, but they still don't fight the urge to reminisce about him/her.

I understand what a wonderful feeling it is to be in love, but you should bear in mind that in order to achieve anything you need to exercise self-discipline. That rule also applies to getting over someone.

In short, if you want to forget about someone, you should cut off the water supply so that the seed dies.

If you are the type of person who lacks the required self-discipline to shut away these memories, you should know the following:

- You don't need to be strong or to have any skill in order to do this. It's a question of practice; the more you do it, the easier you'll find it the next time.
- Don't stay alone, at least for the first few days after the breakup. Remember that your goal is not to recall any memories. Therefore, if having someone with you prevents you from doing this, you'd be better off spending all your time with that person until the first few days pass. The best thing you can do is to pack and go stay with one of your friends for a few days. However, you should not keep talking to your friend about your ex-partner.
- It's absolutely normal to find yourself thinking about your ex-partner once in a while. Don't panic, and try to shut away any undesirable thoughts.
- I know it will be painful, but if you keep doing this, you'll experience a huge change in emotions within a week.
- If you start thinking about your ex-partner, you should say, "*Block.*" Keep repeating this to remind yourself that this is something you should avoid doing. Your brain after some time will be trained to reject these kinds of thoughts.
- Remember, it's not the end of the world.

Stand Your Ground

Sometimes when I give advice to friends about recovering from breakups, they come to me a few days later telling me that they still feel down, and my usual reply is, "When did I tell you that you won't feel down?"

Most people have a misconception regarding recovery from breakups. Dealing with a breakup correctly doesn't means that you won't feel dispirited on your way to recovery, neither does it mean that you'll have a smile on your face because someone broke up with you. Recovery, in essence, means that if you manage to put up with the pain you go through the first few weeks following a breakup, you will eventually stop feeling upset.

Being on a diet is similar; you can't be on a diet without feeling hungry, and you can't break up with someone without feeling down for a few days. In the same way that a diet loses its effect if you start eating greedily, the recovery process loses its effect as soon as you start engaging in the undesirable behavior I mentioned earlier.

That is to say, if you manage to follow the advice given in this book for a few days, you will eventually feel happier, but don't expect to feel over the moon as soon as you start following the various pieces of advice.

You'll undoubtedly feel upset after a breakup, but if you manage to persist in trying to overcome it, all your negative feelings will disappear. The moment you give in to thoughts about your ex-partner, you'll be ruining your diet and you'll have to start all over again.

For example, if you feel upset for two weeks before you start to recover, reminiscing about your ex-partner and listening to the types of media I mentioned earlier will ruin all the efforts you've made to put up with your pain, so you'll need to reset the stopwatch to count another two weeks from that moment. That's why lots of people never recover at all; they keep stopping on their way to recovery and going back to the starting-point.

Sometimes a friend would call me and say, "I'm still feeling down. I want to get back together with him," and I would reply by saying, "You should be feeling down because you're a human being." If my friend managed to deal with this pain for a few days, she would eventually start feeling better bit by bit until she forgot about her ex-partner completely.

People usually doubt their abilities to do certain things, but the truth is you have more potential than you can use in your whole lifetime. According to some research carried out at at Stanford University, the average person uses only 2% of his/her potential. This means that 98% of your potential is untapped.

It's heart-rending to spend your life thinking you can't do what you easily can. You can make use of your potential by constantly learning about what you need to do and by believing you can do it. Why not believe you can do it when 98% of your potential is idle?

The ultimate truth is you can do practically anything, only if you put your mind to it. Whatever you are determined to do is achievable. Therefore, if you want to get over someone, you should train yourself to be more persistent.

Ismail was recently trying to convince an acquaintance of hers that she could get over her boyfriend who she had been in love with for more than nine years. The girl couldn't conceive of the possibility of spending the rest of her life without him.

She believed it was literally impossible to forget about her boyfriend and thought Ismail was being unrealistic for telling her it was doable. Her boyfriend had broken up with her because he thought he had fallen out of love with her and only wanted to be her friend. Nevertheless, she kept calling him to convince him to go back to her.

She told Ismail on many occasions that her life depended on his being with her, and that she life became meaningless when he left her. She had let her whole life revolve around him, and every moment became consumed by lamenting the fact that he had broken up with her and attempting to win him back. This kept on for a long while until she finally realized he would never want her back.

It was then that she stopped calling him, but started going through a phase of intense depression, thinking that her life had come to an end. She spent a long time grieving and refusing the consolation of anyone who told her she could find the right person again.

During one of their conversations at the time, Ismail asked her, "Why do you choose to live unhappily even though you realize he's not going to come back to you?"
She replied, "Because I feel impotent. I simply can't do what you're telling me to do. I can't stop thinking about him or checking to see what he's doing. I can't do it and I don't want to stop thinking about him."

Ismail then asked, "Fine, I understand you don't want to stop thinking about him, but answer me this honestly, do you want to live unhappily now?"

She said "No, I don't, but I can't help it."

It was then that Ismail realized that the broken-hearted girl did want to change, but she didn't believe in her ability to do so. That was the crux of the matter. The only thing she lacked was the belief that she could be happy.
So Ismail told her, "What if I could guarantee that you can actually do it? Would you give me the chance to prove it to you?"

She said, "Go ahead, but I know it won't work."

Ismail said, "I know you think you're doomed to always live unhappily, but please give me the chance to show you otherwise. Isn't there the slightest chance, even a tiny one, that I may be right?"

She shrugged and said, "I don't know."

Ismail asked, "Do you want to try?"

She finally nodded.

Ismail then told her that in order to try, she had to instill in her mind the belief that she could make a change in her life for just one week. They agreed that during that week she would constantly block all thoughts about him.

She followed that rule and fought against every thought about him that entered her mind. It was very hard at first, especially as she had been used to thinking about nothing except him, but her self-discipline allowed her to control her impulses. That exercise of self-discipline is what purged her life of all the misery she was drowning in.

She now confesses that her decision to try to fix her life was one of the best decisions she had ever made. After some time, her self-discipline became automatic, and allowed her to get over her boyfriend.

That girl is just like any one of us. We all have the potential to do whatever we want. The only person who can prevent you from learning to do something is yourself. Make a decision, learn what you need to do and keep practicing it until you achieve your goal. Start with the resources that you have today and don't wait for a good opportunity or a stroke of luck. In order to reach your aim, start right now without thinking about the resources you lack.

Your life is precious, so don't allow a ruined relationship to harm it.

Always repeat to yourself, "I can do it!"

Keep Yourself Busy (It never works)

Whenever I find an article about dealing with breakups, I find the "keep yourself busy" advice mentioned. This piece of advice is not only given to people dealing with breakups, but it's also given to anybody wanting to get over any painful loss, as if it were a magic solution.

So the question is: Does the "keep yourself busy" approach work?

Unfortunately, it never works.

A question you should ask yourself before talking about keeping yourself busy is, "What makes patience so hard, and why do we sometimes find it easy to be patient, while at other times we find it impossible?"

If you monitor your emotions, you'll find that being patient only becomes difficult when you have lots of things to do, especially if you dislike those things, whereas it becomes easy if you're free or if you're doing things that are not mandatory.

For example, being patient during a three-day vacation is much easier than being patient during three days of hard work. This is because when you decide to wait for something your mind measures the difficulty of that wait by counting the number of obstacles you'll encounter along the way. The more obstacles there are (work, scheduled meetings...etc.), the harder patience will be, and vice versa.

It's worth noting that keeping yourself busy can have an undesirable effect if the wrong activities were chosen, which is, sadly, what most people do. Right after a breakup, you become emotionally vulnerable and sensitive, at least for the first few days. If anything off-putting happens during this time, or if you are subjected to a high workload or a stressful situation, you will most likely collapse under the pressure.

Therefore, you should avoid all sources of stress and negative emotions so that they won't worsen your mood. You should never fill your schedule with activities that you dislike, especially during the first few days right after the breakup. If you can take a few days off work or stop going to college for some time, this will have a positive effect on you. You should keep yourself busy by doing non-mandatory activities that you like, so that you can quit them whenever you don't feel like doing them.

Another question that we should ask ourselves is whether keeping ourselves busy is a solution to getting over emotional crises. The scientific answer is that it is not. Certainty, on the other hand, such as the finality of the breakup, can help you get over it fast. Most people don't recover because they keep hoping that their relationships will be somehow fixed. As soon as they find closure, their subconscious minds will let go of the person they are attached to and they'll recover faster.

To sum up, you should start applying all the methods we previously discussed so that they can provide you with the right state of mind for getting over your partner.

You must resolve to let go of the relationship and to stop bargaining with yourself and thinking about your ex-partner. Only then will it be of help to pass the time with activities that you enjoy in order to occupy your mind with thoughts other than your ex-partner. As I have already said, it's not what you do, but how you do it.

If you do it the right way, you will conquer your painful feelings in no time. Thinking about your pain will only intensify it, whereas deciding to overcome it will not only diminish it, but it will also allow you to enjoy your time. Take the "keep yourself busy" advice, but apply it shrewdly so that it can have the desired effect.

And don't start telling yourself, "But there's nothing that I enjoy anymore." *Wrong!* This is the kind of thought you should eliminate because it's essentially faulty.
Don't feed your mind weak thoughts like these; they will only be true if you decide to give in to them. You have the ability to achieve anything provided that you have faith in your abilities. If, on the other hand, you don't believe you can do it, your inability will become a reality.

You can be even happier than you were before the breakup by planning your life carefully. Leaving your life unplanned is the same as planning to fail. Make a plan to have a much better life than the one you bargained for when you were with your partner, and you may one day come to believe that the breakup was actually in your best interest. Turn your dreams into goals and make a plan to achieve them instead of waiting helplessly for luck to be on your side.

Take strides towards your goals. Find out what's preventing you from reaching them, learn about your flaws and start remedying them. Believe in yourself and hitch your wagon to a star. On your way up to the star, have fun and do the things you enjoy.

Is It Love or Is It the Loss of the Relationship's Advantages?

This conversation took place between two friends after one of them had broken up with his partner:

The breakup guy: I'm really feeling bad.
His friend: Why, man?
The breakup guy: I feel so lonely.
His friend: But why?
The breakup guy: Now I don't have anyone to talk to when I'm feeling down, and I don't have anyone to hang out with. My life is miserable.
His friend: But what does this have to do with your ex-girlfriend?

As you can see, the man doesn't miss his ex-girlfriend and doesn't even mention her in the conversation. All he cares about is the loneliness he has to endure. Of course, he isn't aware of this fact until his friend draws his attention to it.

A lot of people are upset after a breakup because of the loss of perks that went with the relationship, and not because of the loss of the partner himself/herself. Indeed, one of the main reasons people feel down after a breakup is due to being deprived of what the relationship provided them with, rather than of the person they were in love with. Below are some of the relationship-related perks people usually crave after a breakup:

- Finding someone to talk to when you feel down.
- Finding someone to share your life with.
- Finding someone to hang out with.
- Find someone to be with on special occasions like Valentine's Day.

Some people feel down after a breakup, but get depressed only on Valentine's Day, for example. It's as if the pain of spending Valentine's Day alone is much worse than that of losing the person they have been in love with.

Although these advantages seem trivial, they are highly valued by some people. On consideration, however, they will soon appear not worth ruining your life over. These advantages vary between having someone to run to when you have a problem, having someone to help one with certain tasks, and having someone who was able to give you free passes to parties or knew how to fold your clothes in a certain way.

Some people even forget about their past relationship(s) as soon as they find another person who provides them with the relationship-related perks that they've lost. I'm sure that you've noticed that people who have lots of friends and a thriving social life recover much faster than introverts who have few intimate friends. The former recover because they find an alternative source of perks, and because they have lots of people around them to help raise their spirits so they don't collapse into loneliness, while the latter remain broken because they can't find any compensation for the lost relationship.

One of the most important questions you should ask yourself after a breakup is, "Is my longing for the person I've been in love with, or for the perks that went with the relationship?"

This brings us to a pivotal concept: Fixing your social life is crucial for the recovery process. Having strong, intimate relationships and a thriving social life can help you forget about any person in no time. What I'm attempting to convey is not the fact that the only reason people are distressed after a breakup is losing the perks that go with the relationship, but rather that it's one of the reasons that makes people feel down.

In each chapter, we talk about a different reason that makes you upset after a breakup. The feelings you experience after a breakup are a combination of these agents. Therefore, if you are able to eliminate them one by one, you won't be distressed after breaking up with a partner.

I bet that by now you know the answer to this question, "How do you get these advantages back?"
Exactly! I can hear you answering the question correctly. You take the time to think how you can open up for yourself another source of similar advantages. You make a plan and you follow it. If you master this mindset, you are bound to become a strong, happy person, capable of achieving everything you desire.

Never say, "Never!" Never say, "But I can't do that." Never say, "Okay, I can try that with everything else, but not with this." Subject everything to speculation and be flexible; if you can't do it one way, think of another way to do it. You should never give in to a feeling of impotence.

What Will Happen a Few Years from Now?

Sometimes we think our problems are bigger than they actually are, but as time passes, we realize that we have over-estimated the seriousness of the problem. Time can definitely heal all wounds, provided that you follow the advice I have offered earlier. The reason time fails to heal some people is that they spend their days doing things that hinder their recovery.

One of the techniques that can help you to overcome a lot of negative emotions – including the pain of breakups – is imagining the future a few years from the present moment. Imagine what your life will be like without your ex-partner. Human beings are adaptable; I'm certain that even if you loved your ex-partner very much, you will have completely forgotten about him/her a year from now.

Try imagining the details of your life a few years from now and you will eventually discover that forgetting about that person is the only certain event that will have taken place. Life will go on; you'll meet another nice person (you'll probably agree with me because you now know that "the one" is non-existent), get married and have children, and if you see your ex-partner somewhere by coincidence, you'll laugh at the hard time you had getting over him/her.

If you feel stressed, anxious or afraid, you should remember that time is fleeting and in the blink of an eye, years will pass. Time passes fast; take advantage of this fact by constantly reminding yourself of it so that you can recover faster.

Another way to do it is to deliberately think about all the wonderful things you'll be able to do in your future without this person. Imagine all the nice people who'll be in your life and all the extraordinary events that you'll live through. Picturing the accomplishments of your future life motivates you to achieve them. More importantly, it will make the breakup appear relatively insignificant. In a few years time, the sadness of your breakup will have dissolved and transformed into a peaceful life, if you decide to allow it to happen. It will have become an idle memory, a mere thing of the past.

Picturing the future helps to inject you with eagerness and passion to turn the life you imagine into a reality. Let me elaborate on how powerful this statement is and how it can better your life. When Andre Agassi was asked how it felt after he became a tennis champion, he replied by saying:

"I've already won Wimbledon at least 10,000 times before."

At first, people laughed, thinking he was joking, but when Agassi explained that he had imagined himself winning the tournament thousands of times, people became aware of the power of visualization.

You see, the reason people become addicted to certain bad habits is because they tried doing something more than once and liked it, or rather the emotions associated with it. Therefore, if a person has never tried a certain activity, he will never get addicted to it. Now how is that related to achieving what you want and visualization?

If you manage to taste the feelings aroused by achieving your goals, you will never become motivated enough to pursue them.

Do you want to fight for something for months or even years without ever experiencing the reward or the feelings of satisfaction you'll get after achieving it?

Here the powerful role of visualization comes in; by imagining what life would be like after achieving your goals, you'll become much more motivated to pursue them.

So how do you visualize your goals? In order for the visualization to be effective, follow these guidelines:

- **Visualize details**: I heard that Agassi once said that he visualized the T-shirt he would be wearing when he won a tournament, the sounds of the people cheering for him and how he would feel when he touched the trophy. In short, you need to visualize the smallest details in order to make them concrete and intensify the experience.
- **Visualize performance and the final results:** Don't just visualize yourself after achieving your goals, but also yourself performing well then being rewarded with the final result. The images you construct during visualization act as instructions to the brain. Your mind will do its best to carry out the instructions you send to it through visualization.
- **Repetition is the key:** The more you visualize your dreams and performance, the more your subconscious mind will integrate them and work on transforming them into reality.

In short, don't underestimate the power of visualization, as it can work miracles.

Visualization is a very powerful tool, which can help you reach your goals if you use it correctly. Many people confuse visualization with day dreaming. While the latter is a hopeless attempt that a desperate person makes in order to boost his/her self-esteem, visualization is actually a way that sparks the motivation to reach a certain goal. There are reasons why we were born with the capacity to imagine. Motivation and achieving your dreams are definitely two of them.

Visualize achieving everything you want, because you certainly will if you believe in it, plan it and give it a go. Have faith, because belief works wonders.

I Won't Find Anyone Like Him/ Her

If you think that you will never find someone like your ex-partner, you are right, simply because you are going to find someone better than him/her. One of the main things that causes people distress after a breakup is the fear of not finding someone as good as the person who has broken up with them. This fear leads to the famous statement, "I won't find anyone like him/her," which, in turn, leads to immense distress.

The first time we do something, it's always without much experience or understanding, but as we do it over and over again we tend to become more aware of what we are doing, which improves our performance. The first time you fell in love, you were still learning the art of finding your soul mate. If you fall in love again, you will become more selective, avoid the mistakes you made the first time, and try to choose someone better than the person who left you.

I am sure your ex-partner was not the best in the world; there are better people living on the same planet as you. I understand that he/she may have had good qualities or special personality traits, but this doesn't mean that there's nobody else who can outdo him/her.

I am not trying to discount your ex-partner's qualities. I am only drawing your attention to the fact that there are hundreds of people who are much better than him/her, maybe living very near to you. After a breakup, make sure that your social life is intact and that you don't stop seeing people, because keeping in touch with people will guarantee you giving yourself a chance to find someone better than the person who broke up with you.

On the other hand, if you stay at home feeling depressed and refusing to go out, you won't find someone like him/her! It's very uncommon these days to stay at home after a breakup and then find someone suddenly coming out of the fridge saying, "Surprise! I'm the one you've been waiting for!" Be more outgoing, live your life normally, and you will find someone better than your ex-partner.

The relative of one of my friends is a very decent woman married to "a most wonderful man," in her own words. They were happily married for many years and enjoyed their lives together. The only misfortune was that she wasn't able to have children. However, they both accepted this and continued to live happily together.

Later on, people kept interfering in their life and asking them if they were going to spend their whole lives childless. Even though they didn't want to have children at first, the husband began to change his mind. Subjected to constant nagging from his family and friends, the husband finally decided to get a divorce in order to marry someone who could have children.
The breakup was very sad; both partners cried a lot and were heart-broken over their separation.

The woman kept talking about how much she regretted the breakup of a relationship she would never be able to replace. She said it would be impossible for her to meet someone like her ex-husband, especially now that she was no longer young.

Looking at her story and her circumstances, it might seem very easy to assume that it was indeed very improbable that she would find someone as good as her ex-husband. Nevertheless, the rules of probability failed to foresee that she would now be married to "a most wonderful man," as she describes her new husband, a father of two delightful children, "Who are filling my life with love and joy," she says.

She feels nothing but respect for her ex-husband, but is completely happy with her current one, and says she couldn't have wished for a happier life. Her current husband is a widower, who was able to find happiness again once he'd met the divorcee.

Years have passed; their children have grown up and got married, while they are still living happily together.

Life doesn't stop and the positive probabilities are endless.

I have heard hundreds of similar stories, and it's true that you do find better people, eventually. Don't pre-determine that you won't; it's more likely to happen than not.

You will meet someone better than your ex-partner; the world is filled with billions of people, and the more people you meet, the more your chances of meeting the right person increase.

Is The Subconscious Mind A Friend or A Foe?

As you have seen, the subconscious mind always makes you see things in a way that is contrary to reality. It makes you think that you are in love with someone, and that you can never live without that person, while in reality it's just your need to compensate for weaknesses that have made you feel attracted to him/her.

Your subconscious mind can make your attachment to someone seem totally genuine, while in reality it may be just a way of proving to yourself that you can do something that you have failed to do in the past. It can make you see someone as your soul mate, while in reality you partner is just another human being who meets some of your criteria.

Having read this, you might now be thinking that your subconscious mind is vicious, but it isn't. The subconscious mind always tries to ensure your mental well-being, which is why it can play some of these tricks on you in order to protect you from getting hurt. Is it better to think that you are in love, or to know that you have weaknesses that you have to deal with? Is it better to think that you can't live without someone, or to know that you are a love addict because of lots of unresolved issues in your life.

The goal of your subconscious mind is to protect you from any harsh truths, but unfortunately it doesn't do it the right way all the time. That's why you shouldn't leave it alone to control your thoughts or actions without supervising its behavior. Don't worry, you don't need to make any extra effort; the information in this book is enough to activate your supervisory capacity.

Recovery from breakups is very easy, but it requires some self-knowledge. By knowing the true reasons behind your attachment to someone – not the reasons that your subconscious mind provides you with so as not to hurt you – you will be able to recover ten times faster than those who cannot differentiate between the two.

It's your decision whether to make your subconscious mind a friend or a foe. It's totally up to you. Your subconscious mind has the ability to do anything that you want for you. It's the most powerful part of a human being, and the most fascinating thing in the human mind or perhaps in the entire world that we know of.

Let me give you a very small example to illustrate its significance. Have you ever decided one evening to wake up at a certain hour the next day, and then woken up the next day only to realize that it was exactly the same time you had decided to wake up at?

Notice how extraordinary this is; you didn't have to set your alarm clock. You just woke up at the time you'd set for yourself, for your subconscious mind.

Just pause for a moment and think about what this means.

You have something that is very powerful and that doesn't work in a random fashion. Your subconscious mind works in a systematic way, and the more you know about it, the more you will be able to control and use it for the purposes you want, thus adding significant power to your already existing abilities and skills.

Every man-made object that you see in our world today actually began as an abstract idea before it was transformed into a concrete item.

Keeping in mind the capabilities of your RAC (Reticular Activating System), you should be able to understand that when you focus your attention on a particular goal, your brain will start to alert you to all the people, information and opportunities in your environment that can help you achieve it and turn it into a reality.

You'll become what you think about most of the time. When interviewing successful people who have achieved their dreams and asking them what they think about most of the time, they say they think about the things they want and how to attain them.

This doesn't mean that you should become a selfish person, as I have been asked about before. Thinking about how you can achieve your goals doesn't make you selfish as long as you don't harm anyone and you help others along the way. Remember that when you make other people happy, you become happy yourself.

Moving on from this digression from our main topic, I'll now go back to telling you that in order to make good use of your powerful mind in order to make your dreams come true, you should focus on what you want and how to get it. The thing that unhappy people do wrong is spending most of their time thinking and talking about what they don't want.

They focus on their problems with not much thought to their solutions. They focus on their worries and who to blame. In contrast, you should become an action-and-solution oriented person.

Always think, "Ok, so what should I do about that?" and *never* settle for something you are unsatisfied with. Work your way patiently through all the obstacles and hindrances to your goal. You should have resolutions so that you can *"focus"* better. Otherwise, you'll be going through life mainly oblivious of all the opportunities and possibilities around you, all of which would be wasted chances.

Your attention is the steering wheel of your life. Knowing this fact alone is enough to make you believe that you can achieve anything you want. When you resolve to achieve a particular goal, you become focused, and therefore alert to anything that can aid you in achieving your goal faster.

Your subconscious mind is your friend if you decide to subject it to constant questioning and understand its intentions. Just like everything else, it's a double-edged sword, both useful and harmful depending on how you use it.

It's like a knife that can be used by some people to make delicious meals and by others to kill. Is it all about the knife, or the way people use it?

Unleash your true potential and use your mind as a powerful friend to help you achieve what you want in life.

The Truth about Love

I know this may sound repugnant, and that you might not want to believe it, but unfortunately it's the truth.

Love is a combination of the following factors:

- The need to compensate for our weaknesses.
- The need to satisfy our egos.
- The need to change the past by proving to ourselves that we can do what we have failed to do before.
- The need to escape from our problems or to fix our mood (external dependency).
- The need for approval and love addiction.
- The need for intimacy.
- The need to be intimate with someone who looks like a person we consider to be a mentor.
- The need to be loved because we miss love.
- The need to get over our guilt.
- The need to deal with unresolved issues.
- And finally unconditional love, which some people claim does not exist.

What's truly tragic is that most people fall in love with others merely because of conditional reasons related to their past and their own personalities, rather than feelings of love for their partners themselves. That is why lots of relationships fail; most partners engage in a relationship to restore balance to their precarious lives, even though they lack genuine affection for each other.

Unconditional love, on the other hand, is the type of love that is unrelated to one's behavior or actions. It's like a mother's love for her child, or man's love of God. In reality, all relationships are composed of two elements: Conditional and unconditional love. The bigger the share conditional love takes up of a relationship, the further it is from being a healthy one.

If you find yourself unable to forget about someone, it is most likely purely a case of conditional love. If this were not true, you would have recovered in a few days instead of ruining your whole life.

You might think that you are deeply in love with your partner, while in reality your relationship was fueled by a need to compensate for the rejection you experienced in your past. The media and your subconscious mind always do the same thing in order to hide the truth from you. The media usually injects your mind with non-existent ideas like *"the one"* and *"soul mate,"* while your subconscious mind hides the real reasons that made you fall in love with your partner, thus making you think that you are genuinely in love with him/her.

People who remain broken forever are those who never realize the truth, and so keep thinking that they cannot find a replacement for their "soul mate." I'm not saying that real love does not exist, but it's very rare, existing in one in a million people.

If you love your partner unconditionally, you'll let go of him/her and wish him/her all the best in his/her life. Your life won't stop there. You'll meet another person that you can love unconditionally. Since we have a mix of conditional and unconditional reasons for loving someone, the more we succeed in fixing our problems, the more capable we become of loving a partner unconditionally, and the more we are aware of how to identify people who are capable of loving unconditionally as well.

Self-improvement never fails to push you forward. You must always seek to make yourself a hero rather than a victim. The more you improve yourself, the more will you tend to love unconditionally, and the more likely it is that you will spot others who love unconditionally as well. Become a lifelong learner of ways to make your life better and a lifelong planner of how to maneuver your way around all obstacles. This will guarantee you to lead a happier and healthier life.

Love is like a knife; it can either be wonderful or harmful. Use it the right way in order to experience its beauty instead of being hurt by its blunt blade.

Living with the right and healthy mindset will make you and your partner feel healthy, unconditional love for each other. If you broke up with your partner because he/she had the wrong mindset, it's your healthy mindset that will help you bring happiness back into your life.

There is a famous story about a very successful businessman in Egypt who made an enormous fortune. However, during the 1960s, Gamal Abdel Nasser, the Egyptian President at the time, started a nationalization program of Egyptian businesses, thinking that this would serve the Egyptian economy well.

Overnight, the wealthy family of this rich businessman became poor. How devastating for them! Since this businessman was then paying for his children's education abroad, the rest of the family had to wash dishes in a pizza parlor. Nevertheless, a few years later in London, they were able to start a new business and made a hundred times more money that that they had ever made in Egypt.

It's your mindset that can make you achieve more than you have ever done before. Always take the chance to learn something new and to cultivate your mind with original ideas so that you will never have to worry about problems or stumbling-blocks. Everyone is bound to face obstacles, but if you are ready with the right mindset and willing to learn how to overcome them, you might even be able to turn them into advantages.

Have the right mindset for love and stop worrying.

Feeling Bad After Breakups

People usually feel down after breakups because of the combined effect of many elements. What is ironic about these elements is that most of them are not even related to their partners. As you've seen throughout this book, the things that trigger your pain after a breakup are related to personal problems and unresolved issues from the past, rather than to the person you're in love with.

Below are some of the things that make people feel down after a breakup. Note that each factor contributes to a certain degree to your general state of distress after a breakup:

- The loss of a good source of intimacy: Breaking up with your partner is the same as losing your source of intimacy. If you find an alternative source, you won't feel upset.

- Self-esteem issues: You might be wondering why you've been dumped. If you realize that that the reason is unrelated to yourself, you won't feel so down.

- Public image issues: You might be concerned about other people's opinions.

- Ego issues: In this case, you might feel distraught until you find out that your ex-partner is unhappy in his new relationship or regrets breaking up with you. If it's true love, you'll sympathize with him/her for being unhappy instead of feeling satisfied.

- Withdrawal symptoms: If you've become addicted to the person you are in love with – which is something that happens all the time – you'll most probably experience withdrawal symptoms. These are similar to the feelings of discomfort and irritability you get after you lose the effects of a good pain killer, which in this case is your partner.

- Addiction to certain phrases: You might miss having someone to tell you, "I love you" every day, or someone texting you to say "Goodnight" just before you go to sleep. If anyone else cares for you in that way, you won't think that you miss your ex-partner.

- Negative emotions are back: If you were using your relationship as a method to escape from your unsolved problems, you'll start to feel distraught after the breakup because you'll be deprived of this escape method.

- Future concerns: "Will I remain single forever"? I only fall in love once every few years. When will I meet someone I can love again?" Concerns about the future are one of the strongest reasons people feel upset after breakups. If soon after the breakup you start a new relationship, these concerns soon disappear.

As you must have noticed, all the feelings of pain are related to your own personal problems and past experiences rather than to losing the person you've been in love with! You are feeling down because of your unsolved problems and your unresolved personal issues, not because this person was your destined partner or your soul mate.

It cannot be denied that some of the negative feelings must spring from your fondness for your ex-partner, but what I'm trying to convey is that if we divide your negative feelings into two groups, we will find that that the one consisting of your sadness over losing your partner constitutes around 5% of your painful emotions. So if you can deal with all the other issues that make up the 95%, you'll feel dispirited for a few days, after which you'll recover!

A one-week recovery period is the result of fixing all the real problems behind your distress and realizing that the loss of your partner accounts for only 5% of your pain.

Still thinking that he/she was "the one"? I'm sorry to have to tell you that there's no such a thing as "the one."

This quick summary serves to help you apply the concepts you've been reading about in this book. Once you've identified the real reasons behind your low spirits, start taking action right away. Don't merely make a mental note, or wait for the right time. There's no right time. The right time is right now.

You should only stop to reflect before you start acting on your problems. Follow the momentum principle, which states that it takes a lot of energy to get yourself moving, but it takes much less energy to keep yourself moving once you start. So, start taking action because this is the most difficult part! Get going and keep going.

The faster you move both mentally and physically, the more energy you'll feel. Since this kind of vigor is exactly what you need at this stage, you should start right away.

Remember that the more enthusiastic you are, the more energy you'll feel to enable you to become stronger and to achieve what you want.

What are you waiting for? Make that decision now!

Fear of Being Criticized

The fear of what people might say about your breakup is one of the most nerve-shattering things about leaving a partner.

Let me tell you a very famous Arabic anecdote about a man called Goha. Goha once had to travel a long distance from one city to the other with his 10-year-old son. At first, both Goha and his son rode their donkey in order to reach their destination.

As they passed through one village, people criticized them for being cruel to the donkey by both riding it at the same time. That was when Goha decided to get off the donkey, walk alongside it, and let his little son ride alone on its back.

As they passed through the next village, people again started criticizing them again. This time, they criticized the little boy for being inconsiderate by riding alone on the donkey and letting his old father walk beside the donkey. "How rude!" they said.

Goha and his son felt ashamed of their lack of etiquette and so decided to swap places.

They passed through the next village thinking that they were going about it the right way this time. Nevertheless, people were again shocked to see Goha riding the donkey, labeling Goha as a harsh father for riding the donkey and letting his poor little 10-year-old son walk!

At this point they were both so fed up with the criticism that they decided not to ride the donkey at all and walk next to it. And you can imagine what happened in the next village, where people mocked them for buying a donkey and not using it at all!

The moral of this story is that you will always meet with criticism. Not everyone will approve of everything you do all the time. This doesn't mean that you should not defend yourself from the verbal missiles that some people direct towards you. Instead it means that you should understand that people will always criticize you, no matter what you do. Don't let their criticism prevent you from making the right decisions.

Expect the best, but prepare for the worst. Stop worrying about something that is essential to human nature, or you'll live in constant fear of other people's judgment. Accept it as part of human nature and learn to face it with calm and reassurance. You should always remind yourself that you've done the right thing.

Don't show people that you are trying to get their approval for your actions, or that you pay any attention to their judgment and criticism. Instead you should show them that you are absolutely confident about the decisions you have made, and are therefore indifferent to their negativity. It's your life, not theirs.

When people see that you don't doubt your own actions, they won't either.

If the people you are spending time with keep hold of negative emotions, you should remember that they contribute to making your life unhappy, and so you should be aware that you might be better off interacting in a healthier social environment.

Reasons for Being Dumped

From all the facts that I've mentioned, you can probably reach a very important conclusion; your partner might reject you because of reasons that don't relate to you, but rather to his/her own background.

This shows that being dumped doesn't mean that you are a bad person. Instead it signifies that you didn't meet your partner's criteria. Since these criteria are based on their own values, beliefs and backgrounds, then you were rejected because of impersonal reasons. Each of the following reasons is one that could have made your partner reject you, and the only common thing between them is that none have anything to do with you:

- A partner could reject you because you look like his/her parent with whom they are not on good terms.
- A partner could reject you because you have different values, even though your values may be better than his/hers.
- A girl could be rejected if her partner's goal is to date a blond girl in order to compensate for his past failure to win blond girls.
- A girl could break up with a man if she wants to marry a millionaire to compensate for her past struggle with financial insecurity.
- A partner could dump you if you don't meet his/her criteria. Bear in mind that his/her criteria may require someone with qualities that are not as good as yours!

The reason people get hurt when they are rejected is that they are not aware of these facts. What hurts most after being dumped is not the loss of the person you've been in love with, but rather your damaged self-esteem. Most people think that they were dumped because they are unlovable, or because they had failed to live up to their partners' expectations, while the truth is that it all depends on the other person's criteria.

Being dumped once doesn't mean you are a terrible partner who is going to be left by every other partner you have, but rather that the life experiences your partner has been through have shaped his/her image of his/her future partner in a certain way that is different from you.

I know an Australian girl who has developed the belief that people with darker skin are much kinder than fair people. She has formed this belief due to certain situations that she once found herself in.

She now only falls in love with people with darker skin. Does this mean that men with lighter skin are not kind? Does the light-skinned man who falls in love with her have to worry about the color of his skin and feel that there is something wrong with him for having a fair complexion?

Let's look at the matter from another perspective. Suppose that you have had an unhappy childhood with a father who you thought was very cold, harsh, and criticizing.

Your childhood was unpleasant because you had to face his negativity and his tough treatment. Also, suppose that you grew up to be interested in the zodiac, and he was an Aquarius, for example. If you strongly associate your father with that zodiac sign, you'll form the belief that every Aquarian is a strict person. Therefore, you'll resolve never to be with an Aquarian, as you were repelled by your father's mistreatment of you.

Many of the Aquarians you reject might be wonderful people, but your criteria are, unfortunately, telling you otherwise. Does this mean that there actually is something unlikeable about them? Definitely not!

Suppose that you admire practical girls who don't usually spend hours in front of a mirror and dress simply. Due to the experiences you've been through, and because of certain beliefs you have, these are the criteria you are looking for. Does that mean that all fashionable girls are to be disliked? Are they abnormal people who need to change in order to be able to find romantic partners?

No. And neither should you. If there's something that you think you should change about yourself, start taking action and learn how you can change it. But if someone doesn't like you, you shouldn't panic. Not everyone in the world agrees with other, or has the same opinions and thoughts. Similarly, not everyone thinks of you in the same way. You cannot meet everyone's subconscious criteria.

What you can do is to engage in constant self-improvement in order to be the best you can be. Self-development will have the effect of raising your self-confidence. The higher your self-esteem, the more emotionally healthy you will be. If you can experience feelings of healthy, moderate self-love, you'll live a happier life and deal better with your current relationship situations, as well as your future relationships. Resolve to always improve yourself.

He Dumped Me Because I'm Ugly

Lots of people mistakenly think that there are universal standards of beauty that are accepted by everyone. This belief is the result of the indoctrination carried out by the media. Some people are in the habit of comparing their looks to supermodels. If they think they don't look like them, they start to believe that they are ugly and that no one likes them.

This is a completely incorrect idea. Beauty is relative; everyone has his/her own definition of beauty. You might see a girl who you would think is very beautiful, while a friend of yours would find her plain-looking. Someone might think that you're handsome, while another would think that you're ordinary-looking.

It all depends on people's backgrounds, not on your looks! If your looks remind someone of a person he/she used to love, they will think that you're attractive. Therefore people's opinion of your looks depends heavily on their experiences.

In other words, if someone broke up with you because he/she didn't like your looks, this doesn't mean that you're not look good-looking. Your looks might have just reminded him/her of someone who treated him/her badly in the past. So they involuntarily associate you with the negative emotions they used to experience when they were being mistreated.

Building on my previous advice to engage in self-improvement, let me tell you something here to help you out if you want to feel more attractive.

There are changeable and unchangeable factors in terms of attractiveness. The unchangeable factors are the things that you can't change about your looks like – for example, your nose, your bone structure, or the color of your eyes and so on. Changeable factors are things that you have control over – such as your weight, hygiene, style, and sense of fashion.

Why some people unconsciously perceive you as attractive is, fortunately, dependent on the changeable factors. The more you improve the things you can change, the more you will be perceived as attractive.

This does not, however, guarantee that a certain person will fall in love with you, because, as you know by now, everybody has different criteria determining who they fall in love with. Going by these criteria alone will make you perceive certain people as admirable and label them as their dream partners.

But this doesn't change the fact that you should always be improving your level of attractiveness. Not only will it make you feel good about yourself, it will, of course, increase your chances of winning the affection of the person you like.

Now that you know that people have different criteria, and you know and that this is the real reason that your ex-partner broke up with you, resolve to work on this issue as I've explained. Do that while keeping in mind that it's normal for people to have different criteria. Not everyone in the world will like you or dislike you. It's all a matter of criteria and preference.

Unconditional Love

Unconditional love is the kind of love that is not caused by unmet needs, a desire for compensation, or love addiction. Unconditional love is the feeling you have for someone in spite of everything.

You might be telling yourself now, "Yes, this is how I feel towards my partner. I love him/her unconditionally and that's why I can't forget him/her." Unfortunately, this is only a delusion, because when people love each other unconditionally, they are never needy. They don't suffer much if they lose the partners they love, and they don't have trouble getting over them.

It's the same as the difference between the two phrases, "I love you because I need you," and "I need you because I love you". In the case of "I love you because I need you," you are usually in love because you need something that your partner can provide, perhaps some kind of compensation, or the satisfaction of an unmet need.

This is the case when reasons other than loving your partner are the main driving force behind the relationship. On the other hand, saying "I need you because I love" means that you want your partner because you love him/her, not because you have an unmet need that he/she can satisfy.

Do you want to know the percentage of cases of unconditional love compared to conditional love? This may sound disappointing; unconditional love is rare to the extent that some people claim that it doesn't even exist. I don't want to be pessimistic or follow people blindly, but I, personally, have never seen one case of unconditional love between partners.

In my opinion, pure unconditional love exists, but it's very rare. In 99% of cases, people have a mixture of both conditional and unconditional love. If the share of unconditional love in the relationship is more than 50%, the relationship may be healthy, but if it's less than 50%, it will not prove to be a healthy relationship.

In a healthy relationship, partners can live independently without being needy or collapsing if one of them leaves the other. Yes, they feel upset, but sooner or later they recover and go on with their lives, never forgetting all the happy memories they had together.

A healthy relationship is not based on needs that must be satisfied, but rather on the satisfaction that is felt when you are with the person you love. To summarize this, the following are characteristics of healthy relationships:

- Both partners are independent, each having a separate life, friends, and interests.
- Neither partner is needy.
- Both partners can survive without each other, but they prefer to be together.

- There should be a strong, intimate bond between the partners.
- Both partners should combat any feelings of jealousy.
- Both partners should be able to recover if they break up within a few days or weeks at the most.
- Both partners have realistic expectations, which are not affected by the messages sent by the media, with regard to their relationship.

Although unconditional love is a rarity, this doesn't mean you can't find it. Here's the rule: The more you improve yourself and deal with your problems, the more able you'll become to choose good matches for yourself and to enjoy healthier, unconditional loving relationships.

I'm happy to think that you can definitely guess what I'm going to say next. Very good, that's it! Plan, believe, and take action.

I'm very proud of you. If this is what you were thinking, you should be very proud of yourself too. You are now successfully developing new, proactive beliefs. With these kinds of thoughts, you can achieve all your goals and protect yourself from pain and depression.

You will lead a healthier and happier life, achieving whatever you want every day.

Welcome To the Real World

The facts that you have just read are neither my personal beliefs about relationships nor conclusions that I have formed based on my past experiences, but scientific facts that most people are unaware of. I am not trying to validate my own beliefs and ideas or propagate a biased point of view; I am only stating unquestionable, undoubted scientific facts.

With the same certainty that the sun rises in the east and that we are now alive, I declare these concepts to be fact. They might not be romantic, but we have to accept them because they are the truth.

Over the years, the media and society have been feeding our minds false ideas about love, relationships, and breakups. Little by little, we have started to believe in these ideas and to think that the suffering they cause us is inevitable. We grow up to find everyone around us holding the same beliefs, and that's why we think that they are true, but we never considered that they could be the product of irrational thought.

A lot of people have built their lives on out-dated ideas and stereotypical concepts, while only a few have discovered the reality of breakups and their associated pain.

You are now one of the people who has been able to uncover the truth, and that's why breakups will never affect you again in the same way they used to. You don't have to worry about turning into an unfeeling robot, because you will surely remain a loveable person capable of falling in love normally, but if you ever find yourself facing a breakup, it won't take you a few days before you recover and feel contented again.

Don't allow yourself to adopt defeatist ideas about life and relationships. Rid yourself of beliefs like, "Marriage is an evil thing that we unfortunately must try to live through," or "Let's be realistic, we can never be happy," or "If my partner really loves me, he/she has to obey me and want the same things that I want." If you build your life and your relationships on these destructive ideas, they will both become distorted.

You know the rules: You and your partner must each pay attention to your individual needs, while taking care not to trample over each other.

Love is a wonderful feeling. Therefore, we should experience it healthily, always caring for each other's desires and constantly improving ourselves.

This doesn't signify that you should be unromantic and dispassionate. This is only telling you to think and analyze why things happen, and so deal with them prudently. For example, if your partner doesn't happen to tell you he/she loves you today, it doesn't mean that he/she doesn't. It might signify a million other things, like his/her feeling down or worried. If you normally and have no difficulty in expressing your emotions, there's nothing to worry about.

Until you find the person that you truly like, I ask you to look upon this phase of your life in a positive way and see it as an opportunity to improve yourself and solve your problems in order to be able to find the right person.

Write Down Your Criteria

How can you make your brain help you find your dream-partner? This is a very important question, whose answer requires that you do something crucial right now. Get a pen and a piece of paper and make a list of all the things you would like to find in your dream partner. The more detailed the picture you draw of your future partner, the better you'll allow your brain to help you focus.

Don't assume that you will recognize your dream partner if you meet him/her. If your brain provides you with lots of options to choose from rather than helping you stay focused, you'll go through life depending on luck. And good luck with that!

If you cannot pinpoint your desires accurately, you may get what you don't want. One way to help your brain recognize the things that you desire is to write them all down in detail.

Sit down and write about every quality you dream of finding in your partner. Mention all the little and big things that are indispensable to you.

You will be absolutely amazed at what your RAC (Reticular Activating System) can do. Don't leave things to blind chance anymore now that you can make use of such a powerful tool to change many aspects of your life, not just your relationships.

Just as you might have experienced before with a new cell phone, car or trend, you can make use of this tool to attain your needs.

Remember to put your desires into perspective so that your brain knows what to look for in your surroundings. It's best that after you write this list that you revisit it over and over. What good is it if you write it, but keep it in a drawer or on a shelf?

After you are done with your list, make a habit of going back to it regularly and refreshing your memory with the criteria you are looking for. Good luck, or we should say, "Good *RAS*" with finding the person you want and who will be much better than the person you were once with.

As you re-read your list, give yourself the freedom to modify it and make small changes to the picture you have drawn of your dream partner. Devoting your attention to this task will better enable your mind to spot your perfect match among a million people.

Of course, you shouldn't write your list and passively stop at that. If you don't know many people, or if you meet the same people every day, you must go out and start participating in new activities where you can meet new people. Everyone must engage in something new every once in a while in order to make new friends. However, you should not label them "friends" before you have spent a considerable amount of time with them.

Persistence and Self-discipline

Self-discipline is the only thing that can prevent you from deviating from the path to achieving your goal; every great success in your life represents your success in persisting.

Deciding on what you want, planning for it, and persisting despite any obstacles and difficulties are what grant you success in doing anything. What you get in return for self-discipline and persistence is courage.

The greatest challenge you will ever come across is your ability to face your fears, which are your greatest enemy, always restricting your actions.

Franklin D. Roosevelt said, "The only thing we have to fear is fear itself," and he was truly insightful.

Think carefully and decide on your goal. When you have done that, persist in following it, unless better options come along you to change your plan.

That same skill can be used to get over someone. Persist in blocking all thoughts of your ex-partner and in resisting the urge to find out his/her news or check his/her online profile. Similarly, you should also hold on to your decision to get back together with your ex-partner, if you have thought it through and believe it's the best thing to do.

Having clear-cut goals increases your confidence and infuses you with motivation. It provides you with the energy to achieve what you need. Use this motivation to stay focused on your goal and never give in.

Developing your persistence will make you very powerful. Don't miss this chance and start working to achieve your goal. If you've made the decision to forget about your ex-partner, you should start right away. That means *right now!*

Make the decision and never look back.

You won't lose anything except for your pain, but you will gain self-respect and the probability of a much better and happier life ahead.

Spirituality Helps?

People around the world are spiritual in different ways and they believe in many different deities. They label their belief differently, calling it Spirit, Higher power, Universal Source, Creative Intelligence, the Unified Field, Nature, or God.

I personally believe in God; because I have unshakable belief that He exists, I have written a book about it called "I saw God," which you might be interested in reading.

My aim, however, is not to convince you that God exists. Rather, this chapter provides you with vital information about spirituality in general and the great effect it can have on our lives and personal power, if practiced the right way.

It has been found that people who believe in a greater power that they can rely on lead a psychologically healthier and happier life than those who do not. Believers are more likely to be contented and more capable of dealing with crises than non-believers. They might have a plan for their lives, but at the same time they are trustful of divine benevolence and wisdom.

This concept has become so widely accepted that 25 percent of American medical schools now offer courses on spirituality in relation to health.

Believing in a Higher Power can help you achieve your goals and find the person you are dreaming about. Many people ask me where I get the faith that I will succeed. Although there are many sources where people seek sustenance and motivation, I strengthen my will-power from my belief in God.

It has been found that being estranged from the divine is what many consider the ultimate cause of human suffering and unhappiness.

When you feel connected to a Higher Power, you become happier, healthier and capable of handling the problems you face in your life easily.

Invest in your belief and remember that if you have faith that your Deity can grant you your wishes, He will not let you down. If your is not request answered now, or if it is denied, you must know it's for the best and that you will be rewarded with something better than what you asked for.

In any case, you must believe that you will get the best there is if that's what you have asked for. When you expect the best, you'll find it along the way, either now or further ahead.

If, on the other hand, you are a non-believer, I suggest you consider reevaluating religion. Don't mistake this for advice to give in to irrationality. On the contrary, you should use your mental abilities to understand any religion. You can never be certain that you won't change your mind. Spirituality may change your life like it has changed those of many around the world who have been able to understand it correctly.

My final advice here is that you should be a believer. I think this adjective is the key that opens many doors. Believing in what you want and what you can do works wonders.

I Finally Let Go of the Nut

The last story that I'll share with you will explain one last important thing that will allow you to make an irreversible decision to forget about your ex-partner. It's a true story about monkeys and their love for nuts.

The way they catch monkeys in India, and also in several other countries, is very interesting. They tie a rope around a heavy jar and tie the jar to a tree. Inside the jar, the hunters put a special kind of nut that monkeys love.

The jar is wide at the bottom, but narrow towards the top, wide enough to allow the monkey's hand to go in and grab the nut. Soon after the trappers disappear from the scene, the monkeys smell the nuts and come down from the trees to get them.

They put their hands inside the jars, but after they grab hold of the nuts, they realize that they can't pull their hands back out of the jars unless they let go of the nuts. They struggle to free their hands, but they keep failing.

The astonishing thing here is that they never let go of the nut. They shriek and make a ruckus, which brings the trappers running with a net and cage. The monkeys, however, keep holding onto the nuts, which they thought would bring them happiness, but which instead cause them to lose their freedom.

I'm sure you have already understood what I'm trying to convey. Yes, we do exactly the same thing. We seek things that we think will bring us happiness, but on the way we lose sight of our purpose, and keep on holding onto what has harmed us. Does the emotional damage you have to endure after a breakup seem like a happy experience to you?

If you have wound up buying this book, you must know that it's better for you to forget and let go of the nut.

At first glance, it would appear that the villager is the trapper, the baited jar is his trap, and the poor monkey his victim. The villager probably thinks this is true, and the unfortunate monkey, if it could speak, would most likely agree.

If you look at the matter more closely, however, you will realize that the villager is not the trapper, nor the jar a trap, because there's nothing restricting the monkey apart from its reluctance to make the decision to let go of the nut. It could very easily pull its hand out of the jar and free itself, if only it could forget about the nut. *If only it would let go!*

I want to pause at the words "very easily," which I have just used. If it were "very easily" done, the monkey would have done it, wouldn't it? I understand how it feels to yearn to be with a certain person, but please answer this: "Is it worth losing your freedom and happiness? Will you be satisfied with holding onto something that you can never have?

Will you remain forever hanging between wanting to be with someone and longing for your freedom?"

It's your decision to make. It's you who choose how to lead your life.
There are lots of people who cling onto the nut and so who are trapped because they won't let go of it. Do you want to belong to that group?

The monkeys' desire to get the nuts is what prevents them from letting go, from seeing the absurdity of their situation, as well as the obvious way out of it. In other words, they are trapped inside their own narrow mindsets. Don't let false hopes or other people trap you. Always be flexible and maneuver your way to happiness. Don't restrict and enslave yourself.

Consider the relationship between detachment and freedom. Bearing pain because of a past relationship and not wanting to let go of it all the same means you are definitely attached. Loosen your hold on your fistful of nuts and imagine what a pain-free life will be like.

I'm not telling you to give up on any hopes you might have. I'm rather suggesting that if your fist is stuck in a narrow jar, you have to be resourceful; resolve to find another nut that can make you happy, and for which you don't have to sacrifice your freedom. Reason, plan, and let go. If you can find a way to get your hand out with the nut, you should grab the chance. If you can't, let go of the nut!

Letting go also means that you stop talking about the lost nut. Like the French say, *"C'est fini!"* It's not wise to continue complaining about your problems because most people don't care, and some are even happy about the fact that you are not. It's only the few people that you trust that may actually care about you, and even they cannot do much for you, unless you are willing to improve your life.

Getting your fist stuck in jars will empower you. Instead of allowing another person to control you, practice self-control and allow the right state of mind to help you achieve your goals.

While you're busy holding onto your nut, which may be making more money, getting a bigger house, working harder or progressing in your career, ironically you might forget about the reason you decided to hold onto it in the first place.

If you don't enjoy the very things you're slaving for, you should start thinking of a way to remedy this. The tragic part is that many people seek relief in alcohol, material possessions, going out, or even sleeping, instead of choosing to deal with the problem.

The solution is simple, but not necessarily easy. Instead of blindly obeying the impulse to hold onto the nut, you need to analyze your actions. Are they serving the purpose of my happiness? Can I fix the situation? If not, you should start planning how to get another nut that can both make you feel good and allow you to keep your freedom.

You are undoubtedly smarter than those helpless monkeys. Why don't you use that story as a premise from which you can begin to remedy your unhealthy situation? .

It's understandable that letting go of even small things can be hard and heartbreaking. Nevertheless, to *not* let go of the things that have damaged your life will burden you with devastating consequences.

Throughout a movie that I once saw, the heroine was madly in love with a man who didn't love her back. At the end, when he started to have feelings for her, she told him that she had finally learned to let go of the nut.

You too should let go of the nut.

Read This Book Many Times

Beliefs are instilled in the subconscious mind because of repetition. The more a belief is repeated, the more ardently will you believe in it, provided that it's in keeping with your reasoning. Over the years, the media, your friends and family have been feeding you false beliefs about relationships. Therefore, in order for you to become convinced of the correct beliefs, you have to see them repeated too.

Throughout this book you might have noticed that I have repeated certain ideas. This was done intentionally. However, in order to further solidify these beliefs in your mind, you need to read the book more than once.

Try to read the book at least three times, leaving a day or two between each time you read it. Each time you read the book, you will indoctrinate yourself with these new, authentic beliefs about relationships instead of the false ones you used to hold.

In order to allow these authentic beliefs to be processed by your subconscious mind, you should give them time to infiltrate your brain, which is why I have asked you to leave a day or two between each time you read the book.

If you read this book more than once, the relief you are currently experiencing will significantly increase. And even if you get into a new relationship and then break up, your new beliefs will protect you from feeling heartbroken for more than a few days.

How to Make Someone Fall in Love with You

About this book

This book is, without doubt, the most powerful book on our planet covering the topic of making someone fall in love with you. Up to this day, I can assure you that there is no other book similar, or even close in content, to this one. The book will definitely increase your chances of making someone love you by at least tenfold.

The book will allow you to easily brainwash someone into loving you, even if he's not interested in you at all. By combining just few techniques from the book, you can make someone fall for you in a few weeks, if not days. Using all of the book's techniques on someone will dramatically increase the chance of making him fall in love with you. One reader even reported that 2 pages from the book were used on him, and as a result he fell in love with the girl despite knowing that it was the book's effect! Some techniques can even make someone become attached to you even if he doesn't like many things about you. With the release of version 5 I started to become nervous that people might misuse the information in the book, as it has now reached a level where it's become a dangerous weapon.

This book is not about intuitive tricks or logical ideas that can be easily guessed like, "be nice to her," "buy her gifts," or "always be there for her," but is rather one that is based on complex psychological principles simplified enough to be understood by all. Most of the techniques in this book are backed up by psychology and scientific research. The techniques in the book are derived from Love psychology, Friendship psychology, Neuro-linguistic programming, Subconscious mind programming, Behavioral psychology, body language, Hypnosis, Physiology, Marketing, and Scientific research.

My one and only aim for writing this book is to help married couples to restore love back into their relationships; nothing more. If your intentions are finding a girlfriend or tricking someone into falling in love with you, then this book is not for you. This book is only for those serious about a long-term relationship, with marriage as its main goal; other than that, I am not responsible for the problems that might arise if this information is misused.

The reason I have to write such a strong disclaimer is because this is not an ordinary book; it's a weapon that can either be used for good or evil. If other books, ones talking about how to make someone fall in love with you, are guns, then this book is the biggest nuclear bomb of them all!
May God witness my intention for writing this book is not to cause harm to humanity.

About the book

I guarantee that applying the techniques in this book will result in letting you lose those unwanted extra pounds and having a great body without a lot of effort.

This book will allow you to permanently lose weight and to have an ideal body shape without preventing yourself from eating your favorite food or going on a diet. The reason this book can help you lose weight in such an easy way is that it doesn't contain simple techniques based on motivational advice or logical tips, but instead it contains effective techniques that are based on psychology, physiology, NLP, hypnosis, and other sciences.

The techniques in this book were followed by some people before it was published and the result was a dramatic change in their weight and looks. All of them lost all of the fat they had, and most of them developed an athletic body shape as well.

Depending on a diet to change your body shape may be a successful short-term solution, but in the long run you will return back to where you started and will regain your lost pounds. I'm not saying that dieting is useless, or that all of those who start a diet will eventually fail to lose weight, but in order to lose weight you are in need of much more powerful techniques for weight loss other than the simple ones that are already known to everyone and that are ineffective.

If you follow the techniques that are found in this book I guarantee that you will lose all of your unwanted extra pounds and have the body you always dreamed of. Losing weight is much simpler than you could have imagined, but you just need to know how to do it the right way, and this is what this book is here to do.

About this book

November 2, 2006
2knowmyself.com making 0.8 dollars/day
August 2, 2008
2knowmyself.com making thousands of dollars/month

This book is a **100% guarantee** that you will be able to make a large amount of money from the internet. If you apply what's written in this book, you will get back the money you paid in the first month from your own website.

This book does not contain information that I have read about somewhere, nor does it contain advice that I believe might work, but instead it contains the approach that I followed to start from scratch and build a website that generates thousands of dollars a month.

The book doesn't contain "A system for making money" like the systems other people sell, simply because these systems rarely work, but instead it contains solid and practical knowledge that can help you make money from the internet, guaranteed.

The book explains every single tiniest detail as to how I built a website that generates thousands of dollars a month, I don't spend money on advertising my website, nor do I spend hundreds of hours marketing it, I just follow an approach that if anyone follows, they will make the same amount of money from their website.

With Google AdSense you can start making money the same day you bring your website online; this book will tell how to set up a website from scratch and how to run it so that you make thousands of dollars a month without much effort.
This book doesn't discuss 2knowmyself as a money-making website, because it's intended for anyone who wants to start a successful money-making website that doesn't have to be related to my website at all. I only took from 2knowmyself.com universal concepts that can be applied to any other website.

Not only do I have a Master's degree in business administration, or several respectable computer certificates, but I also have the practical experience of creating a successful e-business. In less than 1.5 years, a website that contains no more than free articles is now generating an amount of money that a well-respected employee wouldn't earn even after years of experience.

What can this book do for you?
Just like you, I'm sick of all of those people who hype similar products by saying that they are selling the ultimate money-making system, or the get rich in few weeks book.

This book doesn't have the "super proven system" that can make you $30,000 USD a week nor does it have the ultimate proven system for becoming a millionaire in few months, instead it contains realistic promises such as generating a good monthly income that allows you to work from home. Personally, I think that you can generate something like $5,000 USD a month without making a big effort, although the more effort you make, the more your earnings potential will grow.
Even if you only made $3000 USD a month from your website, this will still be way more than the amount of money you pay for this book.

Why you should buy this book?
You will get your money back within the first month. By just applying what's in the book you will be able to earn yourself some good cash in a very short period of time. What a wise investment it is to pay a small amount of money than get a lifelong source of income!
The book contains all the discoveries that I made regarding what works and what doesn't work in the e-business world. It could take you years to reach the same conclusions; I'm giving them to you in one book.

You don't have to have any background in making money online as the book will give you every small detail that you need to make money from a website, starting with marketing concepts, right up to the HTML code you should use. The book contains information that comes from many sciences and disciplines including marketing, management, psychology, sales skills, website optimization, customer service, e-commerce, research methodology, in addition to my practical experience.

The approach explained in the book is very simple, straight to the point, and very practical. The implementation of the ideas in this book is a very easy task as every small detail is explained and supported by clear illustrations; this is not the kind of book where you will find information that can't be applied or that isn't practical enough.

Unlike all other books, the money you pay this time will be returned back to you if you follow what's written in the book, as well as your profits. The money you are paying is an investment, and the return on this investment will be much bigger than the initial amount you pay. The least this book can do for you, is to return your money within a short space of time, in addition to your profits.

Do you always find yourself fighting with your partner?
Are you unhappy or dissatisfied with your relationship?
Do you fear breakups??

Do you wish that you had a better understanding of your partner and yourself?
Do you wish to have a happy and stable relationship?

This book is not an ordinary relationship book that gives advice that is well known, such as "Be nice to him," or "buy her gifts," but instead it gives you numerous methods that are based on psychology which can help you have a healthy relationship that has fewer fights and that keeps both of you happy and satisfied.
If you have a simple understanding of human nature from a psychological point of view, you will understand that invoking emotions in other people is very simple, whether they are bad or good emotions; just by following simple actions you can completely change the mood of the person you love, and the result will be maintaining your relationship.

This book will give you all the information you need to control someone's mood, to calm him down, to have fewer fights with him, to deal with him even if he has a difficult personality, and to prevent breaking up with him.

What is different about this book?

This book is not about intuitive tricks or logical ideas that can be easily guessed like "be nice to him," or "buy her gifts," but is rather one that is based on complex psychological principles simplified enough to be understood by all. All of the techniques in this book are backed up by psychology. The techniques in this book are derived from Love psychology, Friendship psychology, Neuro-linguistic programming, Subconscious mind programming, Behavioral psychology, Hypnosis, Personality type psychology, as well as the psychology of anger, guilt, fear, sarcasm, managing change and relationship dissatisfaction.

What can this book do for you?

You will get the following benefits from this book:

- Maintaining a healthy relationship.
- Dramatically reducing fights.
- Dealing with difficult people who are sarcastic, over-sensitive, arrogant, Type A, stubborn, narcissistic, and more.
- Maintaining love in your relationship instead of letting time erode it.
- Avoiding breakups.
- Getting a better understanding of yourself, your partner and others.
- Learning how to handle anger, sadness, frustration and disappointment with your partner and with everyone else.
- Knowing how to change something that you don't like about your partner
- Preventing yourself and your partners from being programmed by friends, relatives, media or any other source that can negatively impact your relationship.

- Learning how to express your needs, wants and desires without being aggressive and without letting go of any of your rights.
- Lots more!

I Saw God

About the book

This book provides scientific evidence that proves the existence of God, with levels of probabilities that are not subject to debate or revision. The facts are crystal clear and 100% scientific; after knowing these facts, you'll come to the conclusion that there is no other possibility than the presence of a mighty creator who planned all of this.

This book does not prove that God exists through philosophies or emotional arguments because they can be easily refuted, but instead it provides crystal clear evidence on God's existence through scientific facts.

What can this book do for you?

This book is intended for those who doubt God's existence and for those with shaky beliefs about God. Whether you are a believer or not, sometimes you may find yourself asking questions like:

Why did God leave me?
Why is God doing this to me?
Why do human beings suffer?

This book will not only directly answer these questions, but will provide you with solid clues that will prevent the shaking of your belief in God's existence ever again, no matter what happens. The facts found in this book will let you reach the conclusion that there are no other possibilities except the existence of a mighty creator.

This book is for those who want to see God.

What's different about this book?

Unlike most other books, this one doesn't use philosophy, logical arguments or emotions to prove God's existence, but it only uses scientific facts that can be easily understood by everyone, yet which are so powerful as to convince the reader that nothing happens by chance. This book is for those who want to have faith and proof.

The Ultimate Guide to Getting Over Depression

About the book

Be a positive thinker.
Become more optimistic.
Do something new or travel somewhere.
Talk to a close friend.

You heard them all;
you applied them all;
and none of them worked.

If this book doesn't help you feel better ask for your **money back**. By buying it now you will either feel an improvement in your mood or your money back. Personally, I believe that this is the only depression book on sale that offers a full money-back guarantee.

The title "The ultimate guide to getting over depression" was not selected at random or by chance. This book will without doubt help you feel much better, get rid of your depression, have a more stable mood, understand your negative feelings more deeply, learn how to deal with them, and live a much happier life.

Depression and other bad moods are nothing more than messages sent to you by your mind in order to take some kind of action. If you manage to take action as soon as the message is received, the message will disappear, but if you fail to interpret the message you might live with that bad mood for a long period of time.

This book will give you a very deep understanding of your emotions, and then will tell you the best way to respond to them in order to allow the bad feelings to disappear in no time.

What's different about this book

This book does not contain traditional advice like "be a positive thinker," "learn to love life," or "be optimistic," but instead it contains direct and practical advice based on psychology, subconscious mind programming, cognitive behavioral therapy, gestalt therapy, expressive therapy, psychodynamic therapy, and interpersonal therapy, all of which will help you feel much better as soon as you start applying it.

This book doesn't offer quick fixes that last for a few days, then lose their effect later on like "You need to travel," "take few days off," or "talk to a friend," but instead it provides permanent solutions to depression, mood swings and sadness.

The book won't only help you understand those emotions and their root causes, but it will also give you practical and effective steps that will help you get rid of them, reducing the negative effects they are having on your life and preventing them from visiting you again.

This book offers a money-back guarantee in the unlikely event that it doesn't help you feel better. Since I know the book is effective and different I am offering you a 100% money-back guarantee.

How effective is it?

I am sure you have read more than a dozen self-help books that talk about depression, tried various kinds of medication, and asked everyone you know for advice without finding any sign of relief.

I really hate marketing hype, those who overly hype their inferior products and those who trick people into buying things that they don't need, but for the sake of letting you know the truth I have to say that this book will be the end of your suffering, a turning point in your life and a permanent change in the way you view life and bad events.

This book guarantees that your mood will change and your life will become happier as soon as you start applying what you read in it. The book will not only tell you how to get over depression, but it will also tell you how to get over mood swings, how to deal with suppressed emotions, how to control your emotions, how to prevent bad moods, how to become emotionally resilient, how to eliminate stress from your life, how to channel your anger correctly, and how to live a happier life.

This book will definitely give you a strong permanent boost to your mood that will last forever. In short, this is the best depression book you will ever read. If after reading it you find something different, please let me know and I will remove this statement from this page.

To find out more about www.2knowmyself.com books and products please visit
www.2knowmyself.com

The ultimate source for self-understanding
More than 1,000,000 Visits each month

Made in the USA
Lexington, KY
06 February 2019